Franklin P Rice

The Worcester Book

A Diary of Noteworthy Events in Worcester, Massachusetts, from 1657 to 1883

Franklin P Rice

The Worcester Book
A Diary of Noteworthy Events in Worcester, Massachusetts, from 1657 to 1883

ISBN/EAN: 9783337016357

Printed in Europe, USA, Canada, Australia, Japan

Cover: Foto ©ninafisch / pixelio.de

More available books at **www.hansebooks.com**

THE

WORCESTER BOOK:

A Diary

of

NOTEWORTHY EVENTS

in

Worcester, Massachusetts,

From 1657 to 1883.

BY

FRANKLIN P. RICE,

Member of The Worcester Society of Antiquity.

Worcester:

PUTNAM, DAVIS AND COMPANY, PUBLISHERS.

1884.

PREFACE.

IN the preparation of this volume my purpose has been to provide a Reference Book of Dates for Worcester events, which would readily afford often desired information as to the exact time of any noteworthy local occurrence. With this end in view, a large number of items have been gathered, including not only the more important matters which are familiar in print, but also many of a kind not usually noticed in town histories. Among the latter may be mentioned the visits of literary, theatrical and musical celebrities; political conventions, meetings and disturbances; exhibitions, fairs, lectures and entertainments; riots, accidents and calamities; natural phenomena; and many things uncommon and singular. Notes, explanatory, historical, biographical or anecdotal, have been added; and a complete index will be found at the end.

In the compilation of the matter I have drawn freely from the many printed works relating to the history of Worcester, both general and special; from the files of the Worcester papers, (which I have been kindly allowed to consult at my convenience at the library of the American Antiquarian Society); from the publications of The Worcester Society of Antiquity, which have supplied many original items; and from other sources too numerous to mention. I am also indebted to many persons for facts and statements included in the book, some of which appear in print for the first time.

I have endeavored to make the statements as to time, correct; but where so much miscellaneous matter has been brought together, it would be unreasonable to assume that no errors will be found. The displayed dates have been carefully verified by the best authorities, and, as a whole, I think they can be relied upon. The list is by no means complete: a second gleaning—which I leave to some zealous antiquary of the future—would disclose many facts not noticed in this collection.

F. P. R.

Worcester, March 26, 1884.

ERRATA.

No. 102. Supply the year "1874."

" 394. Second line. For Thomas read *Foster*.

" 484. The death of Mr. Maccarty was inadvertently printed under July 10th. He died July 20th.

" 508. For 25th read *21st*.

" 624. For Dickinson read *Turner*.

. A few omissions from the text have been supplied in the index.

. Dates before 1752 may be considered old style.

THE WORCESTER BOOK.

NOTEWORTHY EVENTS.

January 1.

1   **1792.**   Second Meeting House dedicated.

It was located on Summer street, near Lincoln square, and is now used as a school-house.

2   **1834.**   First issue of the Worcester Palladium.

This paper was published 44 years. The last number was dated Feb. 12, 1876. It was at first anti-Masonic, then Democratic, and finally Republican. J. S. C. Knowlton was the founder.

3   **1848.**   Friends' Meeting House, Oxford street, opened.

Previous to erection of this building, the meetings of the Friends were held in Boyden's Block, Main street, south of Walnut.

4   **1859.**   Engine House, Pleasant street, demolished by Gas Explosion.

The building and contents were totally destroyed; and the school-house and adjacent dwellings badly shattered. The cause was a leak in a gas-pipe.

5   **1866.**   First appearance, in Worcester, of Parepa.

Euphrosyne Parepa was born in Edinburgh in 1836, and died in 1874. She was the daughter of Georgiades de Boyescu, a Wallachian nobleman, and Elizabeth Seguin. Parepa visited the United States in 1865 and 1869. She was married to Carl Rosa in 1867.

January 2.

6   **1867.**   Rev. Royal B. Stratton installed pastor of the Old South Church.

He was dismissed April 25, 1872; and died January 24, 1875.

January 3.

7   **1845.** Execution of Thomas Barrett for murder.

The first private execution in the county.

8   **1864.** Great Meeting in Mechanics Hall on Sunday Evening, to further enlistments.

Judge Allen presided. Addresses were made by Maj. McCafferty and John B. Gough. 50 enlistments followed the next day.

9   **1868.** Gen. Abner Doubleday visits Worcester.

Gen. Doubleday was one of the gallant defenders of Fort Sumter during the memorable siege of April, 1861; and fired the first gun in defense of the Union. He subsequently attained the rank of Maj. Gen.

January 4.

10   **1793.** Weaver's Shop of Cornelius and Peter Stowell burned.

This shop was located on what is now the east corner of Park and Orange streets. More than 2000 yards of cloth and stock for 700 yds more were consumed. Loss £300. This fire led to the formation of the Worcester Fire Society.

The Stowells manufactured the first carpets used in the present State House at Boston. They also carried on calico printing and fancy dyeing.

January 6.

11   **1844.** First issue of the Christian Citizen.

This paper was established by Elihu Burritt, and was devoted to religion, peace, anti-slavery. etc. It was published seven years.

12   **1856.** [Sunday] Third (now the Main Street) Baptist Church dedicated.

13   **1859.** Lecture by George D. Prentice, Editor of the Louisville Journal.

Subject: " Present Aspect of American Politics."

14   **1874.** Charles Bradlaugh lectured on "The Republican Movement in Europe."

One of the most powerful and eloquent lectures ever given in Worcester.

January 7.

15 **1800.** First issue of the Independent Gazetteer.

A weekly paper published by Nahum Mower and Daniel Greenleaf.
It was discontinued after two years.

16 **1846.** Skeleton of a Mastodon exhibited at hall in Central Hotel.

It was discovered in Newburg, Orange Co., N. Y. , Length 20 feet.
Weight of bones 2002 lbs.

17 **1857.** Thalberg's First Concert in Worcester.

He was assisted by Madame De Wilhorst and Signor Morelli. Price
of admission. $1. Thalberg gave another concert at Brinley Hall, Mar.
27th, and his farewell performance at Mechanics Hall, April 3d. At
one of these Madame D'Angri and her daughter assisted.

Sigismund Thalberg, one of the most eminent pianists the world has
known, was born at Geneva in 1812. and died in 1871. He was a pupil of Hummel. " In graceful and brilliant execution, and in manual
dexterity on the piano, he had hardly a rival."

January 8.

18 **1861.** Lecture by Professor Ormsby M. Mitchel, the distinguished astronomer.

The first of three lectures on astronomy. Prof. Mitchel entered the
military service in defence of the Union, and became a major general.
He died October 30th, 1862.

January 9.

19 **1837.** A man run over by engine and ten cars.

The accident occurred just below the deep cut on the Boston & Worcester R. R. It appears that the man, somewhat in liquor, was returning after nightfall to his home in Grafton. and at Washington Square,
turned down the railroad by mistake. His horse was killed and the
sleigh demolished; but the man escaped with slight injuries.

January 10.

20 **1863.** Concert in Mechanics Hall by Madame Anna
Bishop, Mlle Marietta Erba, Herr Zochler, M. Arbuckle and
Henry Suck. P. S. Gillmore, Conductor.

January 12.

21   **1778.** "Voted unanimously that the Confederation agreed upon by the United States in General Congress assembled, is agreeable to the minds of the people of this town."—*Worcester Town Records.*

22   **1814.** Nine British Officers, prisoners of war, escape from jail.

They were in Worcester on parole, and were committed to jail Dec. 3, 1813. in retaliation for similar measures of the enemy. They overpowered the attendant and secured the keys; five of them were recaptured within 24 hours. A reward was offered for their detention; and the advertisement insinuated that they had been assisted in their escape by some of the Federalists of Worcester.

January 13.

23   **1806.** General William Eaton, "The Hero who travelled over the Lybian Desart with his little undisciplined army; conquered Derne, and made the whole nation of Tripolitan Barbarians tremble at his presence, passed through this town on Monday last, on his way to Boston."—*Spy, Wednesday, Jan. 15, 1806.*

January 15.

24   **1857.** Disunion Convention.

T. W. Higginson called the convention to order. President, F. W. Bird of Walpole; vice-presidents, Thomas Earle of Worcester, William Lloyd Garrison of Boston, David Mann of Sterling, William Ashby of Newburyport, Alvin Ward of Ashburnham, and Charles Brigham of Marlborough; secretaries, James M. W. Yerrington of Boston, S. D. Tourtelott of Worcester.

This convention was called "to consider the practicability, probability, and expediency of a separation between the free and slave states."

Last resolution: "Resolved, that the sooner the separation takes place, the more peaceful it will be; but that peace or war is a *secondary consideration*, in view of our present perils: slavery must be conquered; peaceably if we can, forcibly if we must."

Speeches were made by Wm. Lloyd Garrison and Wendell Phillips.

25 **1863.** Concert, Washburn Hall : Teresa Carreno, the wonderful Child Pianist.

She is now the wife of Gaetano Sauret.

January 16.

26 **1772.** " In memory of Capt. Thomas Sterne, he died Jany the 16th 1772, in the 76 year of his age."—*Inscriptions from the Old Burial Grounds.*

Thomas Stearns was son of John Stearns of Watertown, and grandson of Charles, the emigrant. Thomas was a housewright by trade; and came to Worcester with his brother John, who was a blacksmith. The latter was captain of the volunteers raised in Worcester in 1748 for defense against the Indians. Thomas married Mary. daughter of Judge Wm. Jennison. He was the first sexton of the town; selectman in 1748; and kept the public house known as the "King's Arms," which stood nearly on the site of Lincoln House block. It was continued by his widow. In this tavern the tories frequently met; and their famous protest of 1774 was prepared and signed here. Two conventions of Committees of Correspondence of the County were also held in this house. Mrs. Stearns died July 19, 1784. aged 77.

"On the first celebration of the adoption of the Declaration of Independence in Worcester, July 22. 1776. 'a select company of the sons of freedom' repaired to the tavern. and demanded that the sign on which was emblazoned the royal arms. should be taken down and burned in the street. all of which was cheerfully complied with by the innkeeper."

27 **1882.** Rafael Joseffy, the eminent pianist and composer, assisted by Miss Belini, gave a Grand Concert in Mechanics Hall.

Before the Mechanics' Association. Joseffy was coldy received by the large audience that filled the hall. and his fine performances were listened to with stolid indifference.

January 17.

28 **1757.** Lord Loudon passed through Worcester on his way to Boston.

John Campbell, Lord Loudon, was born 1705; died 1782. He arrived in Virginia in July, 1756, with a commission as commander-in-chief of the British forces in America; but proving incompetent he returned to England the next year. He subsequently rose to the rank of General.

29   **1778.** Baron Steuben and his attendants passed through Worcester on their way to Congress.

Frederick William Augustus, Baron Steuben, was born at Madgeburg, Prussia, Nov. 15. 1730. He served in the wars of Frederick the Great. Sacrificing a large income, he offered his services to the Americans, and landed at Portsmouth, N. H., in November, 1777. Congress gave him the commission of Inspector General, and he performed valuable service in raising the discipline of the army. After the war he retired to a tract of land in Oneida county granted him by the legislature of New York, and lived the remainder of his life upon a government annuity of $2.500. He died November 28, 1794. He was a man of large heart, ever ready to relieve poverty and suffering.

30   **1861.** Bayard Taylor delivered his lecture on *Humboldt*.

31   **1882.** Death of Hon. Alexander H. Bullock.

He was born in Royalston, March 2. 1816; graduated at Amherst College 1836; member of both branches of the legislature; and Governor of Massachusetts 1866-69. He was Mayor of Worcester in 1859. Mr. Bullock was a finished orator. A volume of his addresses has recently been published.

January 18.

32   **1838.** Lecture by James G. Birney, the noted anti-slavery advocate.

James G. Birney was born in Kentucky in 1792. He was for some years a slave owner; but in 1834 he emancipated his servants, and entered with great enthusiasm into the anti-slavery cause. He was the candidate of the Liberty party in 1844. He died in 1857.

33   **1850.** Fanny Kemble read Richard II. at Flagg's Hall.

Frances Anne Kemble is a niece of the celebrated Mrs. Siddons. She was born in London, 1811, and at an early age performed leading parts in tragedy and comedy. She came to the United States in 1832, and soon after married Pierce Butler of Georgia, from whom she separated in 1845. In 1848 she began to give Shakspearian readings with great success. She appeared in Worcester in 1850, 1857 and 1867. She is the author of a number of volumes.

January 19.

34   **1777.** [Sunday] Twelve Tory prisoners broke Gaol and
made their escape.

They had been sent to Worcester from New York; and were confined
for treasonable practices. They were soon apprehended and brought
back.

35   **1833.** First Patient received at the State Lunatic Hospital.

36   **1865.** Funeral honors to Edward Everett.

The bells were tolled by order of the Mayor.

January 20.

37   **1822.** "In Memory of Capt. EBENEZER WISWELL, who
died Jan. 20, 1822. aged 67.

A member of Timothy Bigelow's company of minute men which left
Worcester on the alarm at Lexington. April 19, 1775. A private in a
company under the command of Capt. Jonas Hubbard in service near
Boston the same year. Corporal in Capt. Wm. Gates's company in Col.
Jonathan Holman's regiment in the Continental Army. He married
Sally Mahan of Boylston. Dec. 25, 1792."—*Inscriptions from the Old
Burial Grounds.*

38   **1877.** Charles Albert Fechter as *Monte Christo*, at the
Worcester Theatre.

Fechter was born in London. Oct. 23, 1824; and died at Rockland
Center, Pennsylvania. Aug. 5, 1879.

January 21.

39   **1793.** Worcester Fire Society organized.

This society was formed "for the more effectual assistance of each other
and of their townsmen. in times of danger from fire"; and the immediate incentive to its organization was the burning of Stowells' shop,
Jan. 4, 1793. (See No. 10.) The names of the original members were,
Joseph Allen. John Nazro, Leonard Worcester, Nathaniel Paine. Samuel Chandler. Ezra Waldo Weld, Dr. John Green. Samuel Brazer,
Thomas Payson, Edward Bangs. Dr. Elijah Dix, William Sever. Theophilus Wheeler. Dr. Oliver Fiske. John Paine, Samuel Allen. Stephen
Salisbury, Charles Chandler. John Stanton. Dr. Abraham Lincoln, Dan-

C

iel Waldo, Jr., and Isaiah Thomas. The members subsequently elected included some of the most prominent citizens of Worcester. The
Hon. Stephen Salisbury, elected in 1824, is the oldest living member.

Previous to 1822, when the Mutual Fire Society was formed, (see
under date July 11.) the Worcester Fire Society was the only organization relied upon by the town for aid in extinguishing fires. Since the
establishment of the Fire Department in 1835, the society has been
maintained as a social body. Reminiscences of its members have been
published.

40   1857.   Hon. Thomas H. Benton lectured in the City Hall
on *The Preservation of the Federal Union.*

41   1861.   American House Block burned.

January 22.

42   1776.   "Voted to make choice of two persons to serve as
civil officers (viz as Justices of the Peace)."—*Worcester Town
Records.*

43   1787.   Gen. Lincoln and his troops reached Worcester to
suppress Shays's Rebellion.

The army commanded by Gen. Benjamin Lincoln, which numbered
4400, left Roxbury on the 21st. On their arrival at Worcester the
troops were quartered on the inhabitants, and remained three days.
They departed for Springfield on the 25th.

44   1858.   Death of Judge Kinnicutt.

The Hon. Thomas Kinnicutt served the town as Selectman and Representative; was Senator and Speaker of the House of Representatives
in the Legislature; and Judge of Probate at the time of his death. His
age was 58.

January 23.

45   1840.   Trial of Kidnappers.

Dickenson Shearer and Elias M. Turner were tried for kidnapping in
Worcester a negro boy named Sidney O. Francis. The boy was taken
to Virginia and offered for sale, but was reclaimed. The trial lasted
three days, and resulted in a verdict of guilty against both. Shearer
was sentenced to seven years in the state prison. See under date September 12.

46   **1853.** Alpheus Merrifield died, aged 73.

He was Deacon of the Unitarian Church for many years; Secretary of Overseers of the Poor; and a prominent citizen.

January 24.

47   **1784.** "Erected in memory of Capt. Samuel Mower who departed this life Janry 24th 1784, in the 64th year of his age.

Capt. Samuel Mower, Jr., married Comfort Learned of Oxford, daughter of Gen. Ebenezer Learned of revolutionary fame. He was a Selectman in 1765. A Royalist Protester of 1774. In May, 1775, he with others was given opportunity, by the local Committee of Correspondence, to join the American troops, or find another in his stead, or be considered unworthy the confidence of his fellow countrymen."— *Inscriptions from the Old Burial Grounds.*

48   **1875.** The Worcester Society of Antiquity instituted.

The Worcester Society of Antiquity was formed to foster "a love and admiration for antiquarian research and archæological science, and to rescue from oblivion such historical matter as would otherwise be lost." It was re-organized under the laws of the Commonwealth, Mar. 6, 1877. Five volumes of Collections have been published aggregating 2248 pages. They comprise the Proceedings of the Meetings, with many valuable papers; Inscriptions from the Old Burial Grounds; the Proprietary and Town Records; Records of the County Court of Sessions, etc. Its valuable library and cabinet are constantly increasing. The Society occupies rooms in Bank Block, Foster street.

49   **1882.** 16 to 20 degrees below zero. Lowest temperature recorded in Worcester.

January 25.

50   **1782.** Protest against Excise on Liquor. See *Worcester Town Records.*

January 26.

51   **1786.** House of Samuel Flagg burned.

At what is now the corner of Main and Park streets. It was formerly the residence of Hon. James Putnam, the refugee.

January 27.

52   1805.   "Erected in memory of Lieut. William McFarland who departed this life Jan. 27, 1805, Æt. 83.

He was Lieutenant in the company of minute men under Capt. Benjamin Flagg. that marched on the alarm at Lexington. Selectman, 1781-82."—*Inscriptions from the Old Burial Grounds.*

53   1832.   "Cold Friday."   10 to 16 degrees below zero.

January 28.

54   1830.   Rev. John S. C. Abbott ordained Pastor of the Calvinist (now the Central) Church.

He was dismissed in 1835. Mr. Abbott was a writer of marked ability, and his productions had a wide circulation. "The Mother at Home," written at Worcester, passed through many editions, and was translated into nearly all the European languages. It was printed in Greek at Athens, and published in Dutch at the Cape of Good Hope. Joseph Boyden, the jeweller, a bachelor with peculiar notions in regard to the duties of women, on seeing this book. exclaimed: *"The Mother at Home! The amount on't is, she's never at home!"*

Mr. Abbott died at Fair Haven, Conn., June 17, 1877, aged 71.

55   1863.   Gen. George B. McClellan passed through Worcester.

56   1867.   New Post Office, on Pearl street, opened.

January 29.

57   1723.   "At a meeting of the Selectmen of worcester, Janu^r. 29 : 1722-3. agreed with Lei^t Henry Lee to Beiuld a sufficiant pound for reclaiming of onruly beasts, s^d pound to be Thirty three feet Square and Seven feet high : of good white oake posts of Eight Inches deep & 6 inches thik : and good oake Rails of 2 inches thik & 6 inches broad at ye Least. all to be Don workman Like at or before ye first Day of March next Ensuing ye Date hearof : S^d pound to be Erected near ye meeting house whear ye Selectmen Shall apoint : for which y^e S^d Lee is to Recive of y^e Town of worcester Six pounds money."
—*Early Records of Worcester.*

58   1854.   Flagg's Block burned.

On the site of the present building of that name.   The fire broke out at midnight, when the temperature was below zero.   Loss, $50,000. In the upper stories was Flagg Hall, which was used as a theatre. The building was erected by Elisha Flagg, who died in 1853.

January 30.

59   1826.   "In Memory of Col. MOSES N. CHILDS, who died Jan. 30, 1826, aged 51 years, 9 m & 24 days.

Was one of the founders of the Calvinist (Central) Church, and one of eight persons who, on the 8th of Feb., 1822, bound themselves to defray, out of their private resources, the expenses of public worship for five years, after deducting such sums as might be voluntarily contributed by others."—*Inscriptions from the Old Burial Grounds.*

February 1.

60   1786. . Rev. Aaron Bancroft ordained Pastor of the Second (Unitarian) Church.

61   1839.   Elliot Cresson, the distinguished Quaker philanthropist, lectured in the Unitarian Church on Colonization.

62   1855.   George William Curtis lectured.

63   1871.   Death of the Rev. Alonzo Hill, D. D.

He was born in Harvard, Mass., June 20. 1800; graduated at Harvard College in 1822; and was ordained Pastor of the Second (Unitarian) Church, Worcester, in 1827.

February 2.

64   1845.   First separate meeting to form Church of the Unity.

February 3.

65   1836.   Union Church formed.

66   1853.   Rev Horace James installed Pastor of the Old South Church.

He resigned in the fall of 1861, and became Chaplain of the 25th Mass. Volunteers.   Subsequently he was connected with the Freedmen's Department in North Carolina.   After the war he preached in Lowell.   He died at Boylston, June 9, 1875.

67   1855. Mission Chapel, Summer street, dedicated.

February 5.

68   1842. Mechanics' Association formed.

At a meeting held Nov. 21, 1841, action was taken to form an association of the Mechanics of Worcester. The names of those prominent
in the movement were: Anthony Chase, Putnam W. Taft, William
Leggate, Henry W. Miller, William M. Bickford, Levi A. Dowley, Rufus D. Dunbar, John P. Kettell, James S. Woodworth, Hiram Gorham,
Joseph Pratt, Henry Goulding and Edward B. Rice. The first officers
were: President, William A. Wheeler; Vice-President, Ichabod Washburn; Secretary, Albert Tolman; Treasurer, Elbridge G. Partridge.

The Association was incorporated March 9, 1850.

February 6.

69   1801. "In Memory of Lieu^t Jacob Hemenway who died
Feb^r 6th 1801, in the 78th year of his age.

Was lieutenant in a company of 43 men under command of Capt. Aaron
Rice of Rutland, who served in the campaign of 1756. He succeeded
Capt. Rice on the death of the latter in camp. Was one of the build-
ing committee of the Old South Church in 1763, his associates being
John Chandler, Jr., Joshua Bigelow, Josiah Brewer, John Curtis, James
Putnam, Daniel Boyden, James Goodwin, David Bigelow, Samuel
Moore and Elisha Smith. Selectman 1764. One of the original mem-
bers of the American Political Society. He lived on what is now May
street, on or near the farm of the late W. W. Patch."—*Inscriptions
from the Old Burial Grounds.*

70   1842. "Charles Dickens (*Boz*) the celebrated author,
with his wife, arrived in town on the evening of the 5th, and
left for Hartford, via Springfield, on the morning of the 7th.
While here, many of our inhabitants called on them at the
mansion of Gov. Davis, where they staid during their tarry in
town."—*Spy, Feb. 9, 1842.*

71   1874. Wilkie Collins read the "Dream Woman." Mechanics Hall.

February 7.

72   1821. "Major Jedediah Healy, Died February 7, 1821,

aged 63 years. Sally his wife died Feb. 1, 1821, aged 65 years.

He was matross in Capt. David Henshaw's company of Col. Thomas Craft's regiment of artillery. A cabinet-maker by trade. He lived on the east side of Main street, where the low wooden buildings now are, just north of the American House Block."—*Inscriptions from the Old Burial Grounds.*

Healy was a noted wag, famous for his wit. "Who's dead?" inquired one of his neighbors, as he was driving the hearse to a funeral. "Peter Smith." "What's the complaint?" Haven't heard any complaint," replied Healy, "I think it gives very general satisfaction!" Isaiah Thomas erected a large stone tomb in the Mechanic street ground, and on its completion, contemplated the imposing structure with some pride. He remarked to Healy that it had cost a large sum, who replied: "I hope you won't lie long out of the interest of your money!"

73   **1861.**   Concert by Stigelli and Carlotta Patti.

February 8.

74   **1834.**   First Methodist Society formed.

Thirteen individuals met in the Town Hall and were organized as a "Methodist Episcopal Society in the town of Worcester." They worshiped in the Town Hall for three years, and first occupied a church at the corner of Exchange and Union streets in 1837. See under date February 19.

75   **1856.**   Bay State House opened.

The Bay State Hotel was erected by a company incorporated in 1853. The house and out-buildings occupy 30,000 square feet of land: the lot cost $38,000; the building $100,000; and the stable $5,000. $15,000 worth of furniture was supplied by the corporation, the remainder by the lessees. Warner Clifford and A. H. Foster were the first lessees.

76   **1862.**   Lecture by Charles F. Browne, or *Artemas Ward*.

Subject: "Children in the Wood."

77   **1874.**   Death of John Milton Earle.

He was born in Leicester in 1794; came to Worcester in 1818, and with Anthony Chase, his brother-in-law, opened a store for the sale of general merchandise. He was connected with the *Spy* from 1823 to 1858, for many years as editor; and was prominent in the anti-slavery movement. One of the founders of the Horticultural Society; and a member of the Society of Friends. Postmaster from 1861 to 1866.

February 9.

78   **1853.** Thomas F. Meager in Worcester.

He was born in Waterford, Ireland, August 3, 1823. As one of leaders of the "Young Ireland" party, he was sentenced to banishment for life to Van Dieman's Land; but escaped to the United States in 1852. In the Rebellion he served with distinction, and was commissioned a Brigadier General. He was appointed Secretary of Montana; and was Acting Governor at the time of his death, which was occasioned by a fall from the deck of a steamer, at Fort Benton, July 1, 1867.

79   **1856.** Great Meeting in behalf of Kansas : Gen. Samuel C. Pomeroy spoke.

80   **1857.** Piper's Theatre opened.

The first lessee was Wyzeman Marshall. A large audience attended on the opening night. An address written by A. Wallace Thaxter was spoken by Miss Mary Hill. The play was *Ingomar*, followed by the farce of *My Husband's Mirror*. This theatre would seat 1200. It was closed in 1866 or 7, and the interior remodeled. It is now the Front Street Exchange.

February 10.

81   **1857.** Dr. Isaac I. Hayes lectured on *Life in the Arctic Regions*.

February 11.

82   **1770.** "In memory of Capt. Palmer Goulding senior, who died at Holden Febry ye 11th A. D. 1770, in ye 75th year of his age. He Commanded a Company at ye Reduction of Louisburg June ye 17th A. D. 1745.

Representative to the General Court, 1741. Selectman six years. Just previous to the organization of the town, he built the house long occupied by Gouldings, which stood on Front street, east of the Common." —*Inscriptions from the Old Burial Grounds.*

83   **1823.** Worcester Mutual Fire Insurance Co. incorporated.

February 12.

84   **1677.** Second Indian Deed signed.

"The right of Pannasunet, a sagamore who had not subscribed to the former instrument of conveyance. [see under date July 13.] was purchased of his heirs and relatives."—*Lincoln's History*.

85   1840.   Democratic celebration of the election of Marcus Morton, by one vote Governor of Massachusetts.

At Brinley Hall.   Isaac Davis was chairman, and Dr. Henry Bigelow, secretary.   Addresses were made by George Bancroft and Benjamin F. Hallett of Boston; and Pliny Merrick of Worcester.

Marcus Morton became Governor by the action of one honest Whig on the returning board, namely : Charles Allen of Worcester.

86   1868.   "Distinguished visitors.   The Superior (criminal) Court was honored yesterday morning by the presence of Maj. Gen. Sickles and Gen. Cochrane of his staff.   The Court took a recess for half an hour, and the members of the bar were presented to the visitors by Judge Devens."—*Spy, February 13, 1868*.

February 13.

87   1783.   Highway Robbery.

Mr. Jonathan Lynde of Petersham, while on his way to Worcester, was robbed in a most daring manner by a footpad, within a mile of the meeting house, on the road to Paxton.   The amount taken was $90.

88   1815.   "When the news of PEACE reached this town, on Monday last, it was received by all with the utmost transports of joy.   The high degree of public gratification was immediately demonstrated by a salute of eighteen guns in each quarter of the town, and the ringing of bells."—*Spy, Wednesday, February 15, 1815*.

February 14.

89   1861.   Ebenezer Mower died, aged 100 yrs. and 4 ms.

"Mr. Mower was a remarkable man to remember events; he could recollect the raising of the Old South Church in 1763. when he was but a little more than three years old.   He recollected the marching of the minute-men under Capt. Bigelow in 1775. and his death in 1790.   As his father was a loyalist, he never engaged in the struggle of the Revolution. although it was his wish to do so.   In the election of President

D

the November before his death, and when he was past 100, he attended meeting and cast his vote for Abraham Lincoln."—*Hersey's History.*

February 15.

90   **1816.** Fire at Adams Square.

House, wheelwright's shop and barn of Nathaniel Flagg, 2d, and Jonathan Knight's store were burned. Loss $2,000.

February 16.

91   **1858.** Benefit to Arbuckle.

Fiske's Cornet Band gave a concert for the benefit of the leader, M.
Arbuckle.

Matthew Arbuckle. the distinguished cornet player, was a musician
in a British regiment stationed in Canada; and deserted to the United
States in 1854. He came to Worcester in 1857, and was leader of the
band here for two or three years. He died in 1883.

92   **1860.** Lecture by Mrs. Sara J. Lippincott, otherwise *Grace
Greenwood.*

93   **1873.** William A. Wheeler died, aged 74.

Mr. Wheeler came to Worcester from Brookfield more than forty years
before, and began a business which developed the extensive foundry
and machine shops on Thomas street, the first of the kind in the city.
He was the first president and a benefactor of the Mechanics' Association.

February 17.

94   **1846.** County Peace Convention in Brinley Hall.

February 18.

95   **1815.** Destructive Fire.

The house, store and merchandise of Samuel Brazer; the office of Rejoice Newton; The houses of Sewall Hamilton and Maj. Enoch Flagg;
and the bake house of Enoch and Elisha Flagg were all consumed.
These buildings were on the west side of Main street, opposite the
present location of the Bay State House and Waldo Block. The loss
was $10,000. The inhabitants subscribed $2,700, and $1,800 was raised
elsewhere for the relief of the sufferers.

February 19.

96   1831. Worcester County Historical Society incorporated.

This society was formed "for the purpose of collecting and preserving all materials necessary for compiling a full account of the history. statistics and geography of the county." Hon. John Davis was president. This society was short-lived, and left few results.

97   **1844.** Methodist Church burned.

On the corner of Exchange and Union streets. This was the first Methodist church erected in Worcester.

98   1861. Hon. Hannibal Hamlin, Vice-President elect, passed through Worcester on his way to Washington.

About 4000 persons assembled at the Western railroad station to greet Mr. Hamlin as he passed through on the 10 A. M. train. He made a brief address in response to their calls.

99   1861. B. P. Shillaber, author of *Mrs. Partington*, read a poem entitled "Life's Bright Side," in Washburn Hall.

February 20.

100   1879. Genevieve Ward appeared in the historical drama of *Jane Shore*.

February 21.

101   1842. Elihu Burritt delivered the first lecture ever given before the Mechanics' Association.

102   *1824* Stephen S. Foster's farm sold for non-payment of taxes.

Mr. Foster refused to pay his taxes because his wife was not allowed to vote. The property comprised 65 acres of land and buildings, and was sold to Osgood Plummer for $100, and afterwards redeemed.

The sale was first advertised to take place on the 20th, at which time the Smith sisters, of Glastonbury. Conn., were present.

February 22.

103   1800. Funeral honors to Washington.

At 11 A. M. a procession numbering 700. including 250 school boys from 8 to 18, was formed at the Court House and marched to the Old South Meeting House, the pulpit of which was draped with black broadcloth. An impressive oration was delivered by the Rev. Aaron Bancroft.

104   **1836.** "In Memory of Capt. Simeon Duncan, who died February 22, 1836, aged 80 years.

Was private in Capt. Benjamin Flagg's company, April 19, 1775. Also a private in Capt. William Gates's company, Sept. 4, 1776. Enlisted and was bombardier in Col. Thomas Craft's regiment of artillery. He marched to Hadley on the alarm at Bennington, with Capt. David Chadwick's company, Aug. 28, 1777."—*Inscriptions from the Old Burial Grounds.*

February 23.

105   **1817.**   Death of Hon. Francis Blake.

One of the most distinguished lawyers of his time. He was born in Rutland, Mass., Oct. 14, 1774; graduated at Harvard College in 1789; studied law with Hon. John Sprague of Lancaster, and practised in Rutland; removed to Worcester in 1802. He was a State Senator in 1810-11, and Clerk of the Courts from 1816 to his death. He delivered the 4th of July orations in Worcester in 1796 and 1812, which were printed. Mr. Blake possessed all the qualifications of a true orator. He married Eliza A. Chandler.

106   **1818.**   Worcester County Agricultural Society incorporated.

107   **1840.**   Signor Blitz, the distinguished magician and ventriloquist, gave an entertainment in Brinley Hall.

February 24.

108   **1827.**   Paper mill of Elijah Burbank burned.

At Quinsigamond. The fire was caused by spontaneous combustion of cotton waste. Loss $500.

February 25.

109   **1775.**   Capt. Brown and Ensign De Bernicre in Worcester.

"Capt. Brown of the 53d, and Ensign De Bernicre of the 10th regiment were ordered by Gen. Gage [Wednesday, 22 Feb.] to make an expedition, examine the roads, note the distances from town to town, sketch positions of the streams, heights, passes, and posts; and collect such topographical information as would be useful for the advance of a detachment. The report of their journey, made by the latter officer, was found after the evacuation of the metropolis. They left Boston disguised as countrymen, without uniform, and passed through Cambridge, Watertown, and by Framingham to Shrewsbury on the old road."— *Lincoln's History.*

See 2 Mass. Hist. Coll., iv. 204; History of Worcester by William Lincoln.

110   **1835.   Fire Department established.**

The Chief Engineers have been: Isaac Davis, 1835-6; Nathan Heard, 1837-9; Henry W. Miller, 1840-44; Joel Wilder, 1845-9; Erastus N. Holmes, 1850-54; L. W. Sturtevant, 1855-8; Samuel A. Porter, 1859; L. R. Hudson, 1860; Alzirus Brown, 1861-65; A. B. Lovell, 1866-8; R. M. Gould, 1869-71; Simon E. Combs, 1872 to the present time.

February 26.

111   **1835.   Powder explosion: 4 men killed, 5 injured.**

The accident was the result of the premature firing of a blast near the deep cut on the railroad.

112   **1842.   First Issue of the "Worcester Waterfall and Washingtonian Delegate."**

A paper in the interest of the Washingtonian temperance movement, established by Jesse W. Goodrich. It was united with the "Cataract" in 1843.

February 27.

113   **1849.   Laurel Street Methodist Episcopal Church dedicated.**

114   **1874.   Daniel Pratt, the Great American Traveller, "delivered a brief but impassioned address to a small audience, [at the Western R. R. station] in which he declared his chances for the presidency in 1876 were improving every day."—*Spy, Feb. 28.***

February 28.

115   **1746.   Day of fasting and prayer for a minister.**

Great difficulty was experienced in procuring a successor to the Rev. Mr. Burr; and considerable time elapsed before a choice was made. A day of fasting and prayer was observed, "to implore the divine direction in the church's leading in the choice of a person to be ordained."

116   **1854.** Mad Dog excitement.

A dog supposed to be rabid ran through Main street, biting horses and attacking several persons. It was killed near the City Hall.

117   **1868.** Murder of Joseph G. Clark.

He was a professional gambler, and occupied rooms in the third story of Union Block, where the deed was committed. The murderers, Silas and Charles T. James, brothers, were apprehended the next day, and were executed for the crime the 25th of the following September.

February 29.

118   **1848.** Worcester incorporated a City.

March 1.

119   **1736.** Bounty for wolves.

"Voted that whosoever Shall Kill any grown wolf within ye Bounds of worcester from ye Tenth Day of march Current to ye Tenth Day of march in ye year 1736-7, Shall be Intitled to a reward of Four pounds, and for a wovls whelp other than Such as Shall be taken out of ye Belly of any Bitch wolf, ye Sum of Twenty Shillings, to be payd by ye Town of worcester, the heads to be proceeded with agreeable to an act of the General Court, page 259 of ye province Law Book."—*Early Records of Worcester.*

120   **1795.** Vice-President John Adams visited Worcester.

John Adams was master of the Latin Grammar School in Worcester from 1755 to 1758, and during this time studied law with the Hon. James Putnam. His diary contains many interesting passages descriptive of his life in Worcester, and of some of the persons with whom he became acquainted. On the 24th of April, 1756, the future Statesman and President penned the following passage in his journal:

"But I have no books, no time, no funds. I must therefore be contented to live and die an ignorant, obscure fellow!"

121   **1872.** Victoria C. Woodhull delivered a lecture in Mechanics Hall, to an audience of 400.

Subject: "The Impending Revolution."

122   **1878.** "Count Joannes" as *Richard III.* at the Theatre.

A large and enthusiastic audience attended. The entire performance was a farce. Wads of paper, crackers, cabbages and other *fruit* were thrown upon the stage, and confusion prevailed.

March 2.

123   **1761.** "Voted That the Selectmen at the Charge of the Town take proper care for preserving ye growth of ye Trees sett out about the meeting House for Shades by Boxing them & that the Inhabitants be desired not to Tye their Horses to them."—*Worcester Town Records.*

124   **1798.** First Water Act.

"The Legislature passed 'an Act authorizing Daniel Goulding to conduct water in subterraneous pipes from a certain spring in his own land, within the Town of Worcester, for the accomodation of himself and some other inhabitants of the said Town.' By the terms of this Act the Selectmen were authorized to take water from these pipes for the extinguishment of fires; and in this small way the first water supply was provided for."—*Report of Committee on rebuilding Lynde Brook Dam.*

March 3.

125   **1740.** "Voted that ye Northrly part of the Town Comonly Called North worcester agreeable to ye Pertition Line formerly Run be Set of a Distinct & Seperate Township if it be ye pleasure of ye grate &'General Court in Consideration of Their grate Distance from ye place of public worship." — *Early Records of Worcester.*

This territory was incorporated as the town of Holden.

126   **1740.** "worcester, march 3^d. 1740. we ye Subscribers being Inhabitants of ye Town of worcester Protest against ye Proceedings of ye Town meeting now held in ye meeting house in this Town for that the Determination of ye Selectmen of Said Town Concerning Voters in Said meeting is not according to ye Laws of this Province in that Case made and provided but they have totally Excluded us tho' Qualified according to Law.   Joseph Dyar, the mark x of Jezeniah Rice, the mark x of Samuell Dunkin, william Johnson, Danil Dunkin, Thomas Richardson, Joseph Temple."—*Early Records of Worcester.*

This is the first of a series of protests entered upon the Records by Joseph Dyer, an eccentric character who combined the occupations of lawyer and shopkeeper. For twenty years he continued to interpose his objections to the proceedings of the town, refusing to bear his burden of taxation, which could only be collected through process of law. Finally, in 1759, he was committed to jail for the non-payment of a fine, where he remained five years, obstinately refusing all offers of accommodation. In 1764 the sum necessary for his liberation was raised by subscription; and he was forcibly ejected from the jail, protesting as he went. While in confinement he compiled a dictionary of the English language, which was afterwards published. For a more extended account of him, see History of Worcester by William Lincoln.

127   1862. Rebel Generals Buckner and Tilghman passed through Worcester on their way to Fort Warren, under guard of six soldiers.

Simon Bolivar Buckner was a graduate of West Point, and served with gallantry in the Mexican war. He entered the Confederate service, and commanded a brigade at Fort Donelson, and after the flight of his superior officers, surrendered that stronghold with 16,000 men to Gen. Grant, Feb. 16, 1862. He was confined in Fort Warren until the following August, when he was exchanged and again entered upon active duty. He finally surrendered with Kirby Smith's army at New Orleans in 1865.

Lloyd Tilghman was a native of Maryland, born in 1816. He graduated at West Point; served in the Mexican war; and became a general in the Confederate army. He commanded at Fort Henry when that post surrendered to Flag-Officer Foote, Feb. 6, 1862. After his exchange, Tilghman was ordered to Mississippi, and was killed in the battle of Baker's Creek, May 16, 1863.

March 4.

128   1803. "ADDRESS Pronounced at WORCESTER, (Mass.) March 4th, 1803. By *LEVI LINCOLN, junior,* A. B. Published by the unanimous request of the Company engaged in the Celebration. Printed at Worcester by Sewall Goodridge. 1803."

This address was intensely Republican in sentiment, and severe in its denunciation of Federalism.

129   1829. First issue of the Worcester County Republican.

Established by Jubal Harrington as a Jacksonian Democratic Weekly Journal. It was merged in the Palladium in 1839. Ben: Perley Poore, the well known Washington correspondent, was an apprentice in the office of this paper in 1837.

130　**1846.** Worcester County Medical School opened.

131　**1861.** Blondin performed on the tight-rope at the theatre.

132　**1863.** Gen. John E. Wool and Staff arrived from Nashua.
They remained in Worcester over night as the guests of Col. John W. Wetherell.

March 6.

133　**1843.** Old Central Exchange burned.
The fire began in the brick building called the York House, on the corner of Main and Market (now Exchange) streets, and extended to the Central Exchange erected by the Worcester Bank about 1804. This building was occupied by the Bank, Post Office, and two printing offices.

134　**1853.** Third (now the Main Street) Baptist Church organized.

March 7.

135　**1774.** Resolution not to use Tea.
——"We rest assured, that however attached we have been to that truly Detestable herb, we can firmly resist the Charm, and thereby convince our enimys in Great Britain and America, that However artfull and allureing their Snares and gilded the bait, we have wisdom to foersee, and Vertue to resist.

"Therefor Resolved that we will not buy, Sell, use, or any ways be concerned with India Teas of any kind, dutied or undutied imported from Great Britain, Holland or Else where, untill the unrightious act imposing a duty thereon be repealed, the former on account of the aforesaid duty, the Latter because we still maintain such a regard for Great Britain, as to be unwilling to promote the interest of a rival."— *Worcester Town Records.*

136　**1804.** Worcester Bank chartered.

March 8.

137　**1762.** Voted to build a New Meeting House.
The result was the erection, in 1763, of the present Old South Church.

E

March 9.

138   **1869.** Music Hall or New Theatre dedicated.

Now the Worcester Theatre. The play on the opening night was The Lady of Lyons, by the Boston Theatre Company.

139   **1878.** Col. Robert G. Ingersoll delivered his lecture on "Skulls," in Mechanics Hall.

March 10.

140   **1848.** The Remains of Ex-President John Quincy Adams passed through Worcester to Boston.

The funeral train made a short stop at Washington square, where some thousands had assembled. Minute guns were fired and bells tolled. Ex-Governor Levi Lincoln addressed the Congressional Committee in charge of the remains, and the Hon. Isaac E. Holmes, of South Carolina, replied in a most beautiful and eloquent strain.

141   **1854.** Indignation meeting in consequence of the death of Maj. John H. Knight.

He was formerly station master at the Norwich depot. He received a fatal contusion on the head by falling down stairs, as was alleged, in a saloon at Washington square; but the verdict of the coroner's jury was that his death was caused by a blow from a heavy weapon in the hands of some unknown person. The meeting was called in the interest of temperance, and to take measures to suppress the rum traffic.

March 11.

142   **1854.** Mass Meeting to protest against the passage of the Kansas-Nebraska bill.

At the City Hall. Speeches were made by Peter C. Bacon, Rev. Elam Smalley, Dwight Foster, Charles Allen, Rev. Horace James, Eli Thayer and Homer B. Sprague.

143   **1860.** Samuel Jennison died, aged 72.

He was for thirty years cashier of the Worcester Bank; twenty years treasurer of the Worcester County Institution for savings; and ten years treasurer of the State Lunatic Asylum: also treasurer of the American Antiquarian Society; and of the Corporation of Rural Cemetery. He was an antiquary of some note. His residence was on Pearl Street.

March 12.

144   1828.   Central Bank incorporated.

145   1830.   Worcester County Athenæum incorporated.

The intention was to form a library for general use. Thirty-four proprietors purchased shares at $25 each, and organized with Rev. George Allen as president; Frederick W. Paine as treasurer; and William Lincoln, secretary. Some thousands of volumes were collected; but the association was discontinued after a few years, and the library turned over to the American Antiquarian Society.

146   1868.   Concert by Leopold De Meyer, with Madame Gagzaniga, Signor Ardarani, Bernhard Listemann and Samuel Warren.

March 13.

147   1802.   Gov. Caleb Strong in Worcester.

He arrived from Boston on Saturday the 13th, remained over Sunday, and departed on Monday for his home in Northampton.

Caleb Strong was Governor of Massachusetts from 1800 to 1807; and from 1812 to 1816. He had previously been a Justice of the Supreme Court and United States Senator. He was an ultra Federalist, and entered into the wellnigh treasonable actions of his party during the last war with Great Britain. Fortified by a decision of the Chief Justice, he refused to comply with President Madison's requisition for troops, and openly defied the Government at Washington. Practically, this was nullification: the doctrine of secession had previously been proclaimed by a Massachusetts Representative in Congress. Governor Strong died November 7th, 1819, aged 74.

148   1883.   Dr. Damrosch and Orchestra, with Teresa Carreno and Isadora Martinez gave a Grand Concert in Mechanics Hall.

The most finished orchestral performance ever listened to in Worcester.

March 14.

149   1737.   "Whearas much damige hath been Don by black birds, blew Jays and wood peckers by Taring up Indian Corn & Devouring yᵉ Same in yᵉ fields, &c., therefore

"Voted that Every person belonging to this Town that Shall from the first Day of april to the last Day of may next Kill any black birds, and for one year next coming who Shall Kill any wood Peckers or blew Jays & bring the heads thereof to yᵉ Town Tresurer, Town Clerk or either of yᵉ Selectmen Shall be Intitled to a Premiam or Reward of three pence for Each head, producing a Certificate thereof, & that yᵉ Same be Consumed to ashes."—*Early Records of Worcester.*

150   **1861.** Orson N. Heath lectured in Mechanics Hall on "Success in Life."

Heath kept the *Poetical Exchange,* a second-hand furniture store, under the Bay State House, Exchange street side.

151   **1874.** Remains of Charles Sumner passed through Worcester.

3000 persons assembled at Washington square. Bells were tolled while the funeral train was within the city limits.

March 15.

152   **1848.** Gen. Sam Houston in Worcester.

Gen. Houston of Texas arrived from Providence in the afternoon, and remained at the American House about an hour. during which time he was visited by numerous citizens. He left in the evening on the steamboat train for New York.

153   **1867.** Dedication of the new Orphans' Home.

At the corner of Main and Benefit streets. The old Home, which was given to the Children's Friend Society by John W. Lincoln, was on Shrewsbury street. east of the Pine Meadow settlement.

March 16.

154   **1751.** Order to build a new Court House.

Dimensions 36 by 40 feet. It was removed on wheels to the present Trumbull square at the lower end of Park street, about 1801, and converted into the mansion long occupied by the late George A. Trumbull.

155   **1842.** Sampson V. S. Wilder committed to jail for debt.

Sampson Vryling Stoddard Wilder resided in Europe for many years as a commercial agent, and accumulated a large fortune with which he returned to America, and retired to a princely estate in Bolton, near his birthplace. Here he entertained LaFayette in 1824. In the financial crisis of 1837 his wealth was suddenly swept away; and consequent troubles followed, which finally brought him to Worcester Jail, a prisoner for debt. He was released by his creditor, June 14, 1842. Mr. Wilder was a man of public spirit and generous benevolence. He died at Elizabeth, N. J., in 1865, aged 85.

156 **1873.** Heavy Gale : staging at St. Paul's Church, brick walls, and chimneys in different parts of the city blown down.

March 17.

157 **1790.** "Sacred to the memory of Deacon Jacob Chamberlain who departed this life March ye 17th 1790 in the 71st year of his age. Who fulfilled the office of a Deacon in the Church of Christ in Worcester for about 28 years with Satisfaction to the Church and Honour to himself. He was possess'd of good natural Abilities Useful in the Society of which he was a member Instructive and entertaining in conversation Compassionate to the afflicted Given to hospitality—sound in the faith· And now, we trust, has entered into his Eternal Rest.

Deacon Jacob Chamberlain was born at a place called Oak Hill in Newton, Nov. 28, 1719. He married Lydia Stone of Newton in early life, when he removed to Worcester and settled on the farm now (1877) occupied by the widow of the late Marshall Flagg, where he lived during the residue of his life. By his first wife he had nine children, viz: John, Sarah, Thaddeus, Lydia, Jacob, Susannah, Abigail, Mary and William. By a second wife (widow of Abel Heywood, who was son of Maj. Heywood of ancient memory in this town) he had one daughter, Nancy.

Deacon Chamberlain was selectman of the town, 1761. A tory protester of 1774, numbered among the internal enemies by the Committee of Correspondence in 1775, and disarmed by that committee."
—*Inscriptions from the Old Burial Grounds.*

158 **1806.** Worcester Turnpike Company incorporated.
Air line to Boston.

March 18.

159 1776. "Capt. James Goodwin & M^r. Daniel Bigelow Ju^r. was Chosen a Committee to Inspect the behavior of such persons as tarry in the meeting House on Sabbath Days between meetings and if they shall discover any misbehavior that they inform lawfull authority of the same that offenders may be punnished."—*Worcester Town Records.*

160 1825. "In Memory of Mr. CURTIS FOWLE, who died March 18, 1825, aged 80.

"An Englishman by birth—came to this Country—joined the American army in 1775, and faithfully served during the war.

"He married Susannah Shedd. January 23, 1785.

"From the SPY. March 23. 1825. 'Died 18th inst. Mr. Curtis Fowle aged 80. He was an Englishman by birth. came to this country about the year 1766, on board a British Frigate. from which he deserted. In 1775 he joined the American Army, in which he faithfully served during the whole Revolutionary war.' "—*Inscriptions from the Old Burial Grounds.*

March 19.

161 1845. Rev. George P. Smith installed Pastor of the Old South Church.

He died Sept. 3, 1852.

162 1857. Mechanics Hall dedicated.

The exercises began at 2 P. M. Henry S. Washburn delivered an address, followed by remarks from Lieut. Gov. Benchley. Mayor Richardson, Ex-Gov. Lincoln, A. H. Bullock and others. In the evening there was a concert by Adelaide Phillips and the Boston Orchestral Union. Carl Zerrahn. leader.

In 1854 Ichabod Washburn gave $10,000 towards the purchase of land and the erection of a building, and an equal amount was subscribed by others. The Waldo lot was purchased for $30,000. The total cost of the building was $140, 129, 51. Elbridge Boyden was the architect.

March 20.

163 1786. "Voted to sell the Ministerial and School Lands

lying east and near Capt. Palmer Goulding's and that it be sold at Public Vendue."— *Town Records.*

Timothy Paine Esq., Capt. Samuel Brooks, Col. Timothy Bigelow, Joseph Wheeler, Esq., and Dr. Elijah Dix were chosen a committee to sell the same, and were empowered to execute good and sufficient deed or deeds to the purchasers. "This parcel as surveyed out by Capt. John Pierce, May 5th, 1786, contained thirteen and one quarter acres and twenty-three rods; and the [Mechanic street] burial ground lot was selected near the center of the plot." The land was sold in lots as follows: "Lot No. 1, containing 1 3-4 acres and sum rods, sold to Daniel Goulding for the sum of 20 pounds; lot No. 2, containing 121 rods, sold to Silas Harrington for the sum of 19 pounds, 10 shillings, and by him released to Jno. Jacob Wagoner who sold ye same to Jacob Miller, ye present possessor; lot No. 3, containing 110 rods, sold to Benj. Converse for the sum of 20 pounds, 9 shillings, which his guardean has since sold to Ignatius Goulding; lot No. 4, containing 82 rods sold to Nathan Patch who forfited his earnest money, and the same has since been sold to William Goulding for the sum of 15 pounds, 10 shillings; lot No. 5, containing 5 3-4 acres and 14 rods, sold to Jonathan Gates who forfited his earnest money, and the same has since been sold to Abel Stowell for the sum of 27 pounds, 15 shillings; lot No. 6, containing 2 acres and 58 rods, sold to Ignatius Goulding for the sum of 42 pounds, 10 shillings."—*Old Burial Grounds of Worcester.*

164   1855. Concert in the City Hall by Paul Julien, Adelina Patti and August Gockel.

March 21.

165   1861. Great Snowstorm: drifts 5 to 12 feet high. Two chimneys on Lincoln House blown over, breaking through the roof of a room where servant girls were sleeping.

166   1873. Joseph Jefferson as *Rip Van Winkle*, at the theatre.

March 22.

167   1814. "To the memory of Col. PHINEAS JONES, died March 22, 1814, Æt. 66

"Married Katharine Gates, April 21st, 1772. Was sergeant in Capt. David Chadwick's company that marched to Hadley on the alarm at Bennington, Aug. 28, 1777.

"Was chief marshal at the military celebration on the anniversary of the Declaration of Independence in Worcester, 1789. Selectman in 1796-7. He kept the Old Jones Tavern near New Worcester."—*Inscriptions from the Old Burial Grounds.*

March 23.

168   1827. "In Memory of Daniel Clapp, Esq. who died March 23, 1827, aged 87.

"Was one of fifteen jurors who refused, April 19, 1774. to serve under Chief Justice Peter Oliver. because the last House of Representatives had impeached him for receiving his salary from the English Crown.
  "Was Register of Deeds from 1784 to 1816.
  "He lived on what is now the corner of Main and Park streets"—*Inscriptions from the Old Burial Grounds.*

169   1857. Frederick Douglass addressed a meeting in the City Hall, at the close of which brief remarks were made by Capt. John Brown, of Kansas notoriety.

170   **1868.** Charles Dickens read his *Christmas Carol* and the Trial from *Pickwick*, in Mechanics Hall.
  A large audience was present. The price of tickets was $2.

March 24.

171   1853. Death of Benjamin F. Newton.
  Mr. Newton was District Attorney at the time of his death. He possessed excellent abilities as a lawyer. His age was 32.

172   **1878.** Death of the Rev. Seth Sweetser, D. D.
  He was born in Newburyport, March 15. 1807. He was installed pastor of the Central Church in 1838. and passed the remainder of his life in Worcester. Dr. Sweetser was an Overseer of Harvard College; was connected with the management of other educational institutions; and was a prominent member of the American Antiquarian Society.

March 25.

173   1833. Quinsigamond Bank incorporated.

174   **1857.** John Brown addressed a meeting in the City Hall.

FIRST UNITARIAN CHURCH.

A. D. 1883.

March 26.

175   1851.   New Unitarian Church dedicated.

The present edifice on Court Hill. It is of brick covered with mastic in squares to represent stone work, and cost about $25.000, which sum was raised by the sale of pews. Joel Wilder, mason, was the builder.

176   1866.   Matilda Heron in *Camille*, at the Theatre.

March 27.

177   1860.   Free Public Library opened.

Accounts were opened with two hundred persons, and 36 catalogues were sold on the first day. The library, at this time, occupied the upper story of Bank Block, Foster street.

March 28.

178   1827.   Rev. Alonzo Hill ordained.

179   1855.   P. T. Barnum lectured in the City Hall on *Money Making*.

180   1876.   Old Men's Home established.

March 29.

181   1728.   "Voted that ye Incourigment for killing of Ratle Snakes in S^d Town Shall be three pence for every Ratle Snakes Taile or ratle So killed & brought to one or more of ye Selectmen, who are directed to recive ye Same."—*Early Records.*

182   1861.   John S. Rarey, the Horse Tamer, with his celebrated horse *Cruiser*, gave an exhibition in Mechanics Hall.

March 30.

183   1876.   Lynde Brook Dam carried away by a freshet.

"Dams, bridges, mills, roads and dwellings were swept away; but no lives were lost. . . . . About 5000 feet of the Boston & Albany R. R. track was taken off, and the embankment washed away. . . . At one time the water came within 50 feet of the Horse Car track at New Worcester." The aggregate damages paid by the city, including the cost of the new dam, amounted to $227,000.

F

March 31.

184   **1790.   Death of Col. Timothy Bigelow.**

He was born in Worcester, August 12, 1739. His father, Daniel Bigelow, who married Elizabeth Whitney, came from Watertown, and settled in the south part of Worcester, now included in Auburn, where he died at the age of 92. Timothy was a blacksmith by trade. He became an ardent patriot; was chosen to command the minute men; and marched with his company to Cambridge on the alarm, April 19, 1775. He was a volunteer in the expedition against Quebec, where he was made a prisoner. He was appointed to command the 15th Mass. regiment; joined the northern army, and assisted in capturing Burgoyne. After the war he obtained a grant of land in Vermont, and founded the town of Montpelier. He returned to Worcester in impoverished circumstances, and died while a prisoner for debt. The entry in the Jail Book is that he was discharged "*By Deth.*" See under date April 19.

185   **1857.   John B. Gough lectured in the New Hall for the benefit of the Mechanics Association.**

The largest lecture audience that had ever assembled in Worcester. $300. was realized.

186   **1871.   Worcester Choral Union incorporated.**

187   **1882.   Visit of the Zuni Indians.**

They were accompanied by Mr. Frank H. Cushing of the Smithsonian Institution; and numbered six chiefs of high rank. They visited the High School, Antiquarian Hall, the Wire Works and other manufactories, and the Jail.

188   **1883.   Rev. George Allen died, aged 91 years, 2 months.**

He was born in a house that stood on the north corner of Main and School streets, February 1, 1792. His father, the Hon. Joseph Allen, was Clerk of the Courts and afterwards a Member of Congress; his paternal grandmother was a sister of Samuel Adams. George Allen graduated at Yale College in 1813; was minister at Shrewsbury from 1823 to 1840; and chaplain at the State Lunatic Hospital from 1840 to 1872. Mr. Allen took part in the anti-slavery agitation, contributing much to the press, and writing several pamphlets that attracted considerable attention. He was the author of the celebrated Free Soil resolution of 1848. (See under dates June 21 and Dec. 5.)   He was a fine scholar, and a writer of wonderful power.

April 1.

189   **1851.**   First Daily Morning Transcript.

This paper had no connection with the "Daily Transcript" published in 1845. Julius L. Clarke was the first editor. It was at first neutral in politics, then Whig. and finally Republican. The name was changed to "Worcester Evening Gazette." Jan. 1. 1866. The several editors of the "Transcript" after Mr. Clarke, were Charles E. Stevens, Edwin Bynner. J. B. D. Cogswell, Z. K. Pangborn, William R. Hooper and Caleb A. Wall.

190   **1858.**   Rufus Choate lectured in Mechanics Hall on *Hamilton and Burr*.

191   **1868.**   Henry W. Shaw, alias *Josh Billings*, lectured in Mechanics Hall on *Milk*.

192   **1873.**   First issue of The Worcester Daily Press.

A Democratic Journal. The last number was dated April 27. 1878, when the subscription list was transferred to the Spy. This enterprize was disastrous to those concerned; and several prominent Democrats, it is said, were "out of pocket" $75.000 in the aggregate.

193   **1883.**   Hon. Isaac Davis died, aged 83 years, 10 months.

He was born in Northborough. June 2, 1799. He graduated at Brown University in 1822; and took up his residence in Worcester the same year. He was admitted to the bar in 1825. He was Chief Engineer of the Fire Department in 1835; State Senator, 1844; and Mayor in 1856, 1858. and 1861. He was the Democratic candidate for Governor in 1846 and 1847; and Delegate to all the National Democratic Conventions from 1828 to 1860. He acquired large wealth, mostly by real estate transactions.

April 2.

194   **1731.**   Worcester County incorporated.

The act took effect the 10th of the following July.

April 3.

195   **1865.**   News of the fall of Richmond received.

Bells were rung and 100 guns fired on the Common and at Quinsigamond; the State Guards paraded; and there was an illumination in the evening.

April 4.

196   **1726.** First Schoolmaster hired : "We yᵉ Subscribers Doe hearby Covenant & agree with mr. Jonas Rice to be yᵉ Schoole master for Sᵈ Town of worcester and to teach Such Children & Youth as any of yᵉ Inhabitents Shall Send to him : to read & to write as yᵉ Law Directs, &c :   And to keep Such Schoole untill yᵉ fifteenth Day of December next Ensuing yᵉ Date hearof : Sᵈ Schoole to [be] Supported at the Towns Charge.   ·

Nath¹¹ Moore
Daniel Heywood } *Selectmen*
Benjᵃ Flagg } *of Worcester.*"
James Taylor

—Early Records.

197   **1831.** Death of Isaiah Thomas.

He was born in Boston, January 19. 1749. The *Massachusetts Spy* was established by him in 1771, and became the organ of the patriots. A short time before the battle of Lexington, he removed his press and types to Worcester, where, after the war, he carried on the most extensive publishing business in the country. He was Postmaster from 1776 to 1801. Founder and patron of the American Antiquarian Society; and author of a valuable History of Printing.

198   **1879.** Edouard Remenyi, the celebrated violinist, at Mechanics Hall.

199   **1881.** Sarah Bernhardt as *Marguerite Gautier* in *Camille*, at the Theatre.

Prices of seats, $1, $2 and $3 according to location.

April 5.

200   **1860.** Death of Hon. Abijah Bigelow.

He was born in Westminster. Dec. 5. 1775. Graduated at Dartmouth College. 1795. Represented this district in Congress from 1810 to 1815. Clerk of the Courts. 1817 to 1833. He lived for many years at the corner of Front and Church streets. in the house recently removed to make way for Jonas G. Clarke's block.

201   **1872.** Escape of Sam Perris, one of the Grafton Bank robbers, from the Worcester Jail.

Sam Perris, otherwise "Worcester Sam" was awaiting trial for robbing the Grafton Bank, Oct. 25, 1870, by which act he and his associates secured $180,000. Perris effected his escape from the fourth story window at the north end of the jail, forcing the bars by which it was guarded with a powerful jack screw furnished by confederates outside, and which he drew up with a rope. He then let himself down along the dead wall, a distance of 80 feet. He has never been recaptured.

April 6.

202   1777.

"Memento mori

Under this covring sleeps
the mouldring Bons
Ah - tis the frail Remains
of Captⁿ. William Jones
On April 6ᵗʰ 1777
Death him Remov'd
from toils of Earth
to joys of Heaven.
Æt 51

"Generally known as 'Tory Jones.' Kept a tavern on what is now Main street, nearly opposite Chatham street. His house was a favorite resort for the tories of Worcester in the early days of the Revolution. Capt. Jones entertained Capt. Brown and Ensign De Bernicre of his majesty's troops ordered here by Gen. Gage in the spring of 1775. [See No. 109] Gen. Gage at that time contemplated erecting a fortress on Chandler Hill. William Jones married Sarah Curtis, daughter of John Curtis." —*Inscriptions from the Old Burial Grounds.*

April 7.

203   1783.   "Whereas a number of persons have manifested a disposition to Set out trees for Shades near the Meeting house & elsewhere about the Center of this Town, & the Town being desirous of encouraging Such a measure which will be beneficial as well as ornamental

"Therefore Voted, that any person being an Inhabitant of this Town, who shall injure or destroy such trees so set out, shall pay a fine not exceeding twenty shillings for every offence, to be disposed of to the use of the poor of the Town." *Worcester Town Records.*

204   **1865.**   Illumination for Union victories.

205   **1874.**   All Saints [Episcopal] Church burned.

Pearl street, on the site now occupied by the fine stone residence built for Dr. Bull. This church was of wood, built in 1847. The new All Saints Church, at the corner of Pleasant and Irving streets, was consecrated January 4th, 1877.

April 8.

206   **1848.**   First City Election.

Ex-Gov. Lincoln and Rev. Rodney A. Miller, "a respected Divine, ran neck and neck" for the office of Mayor. Gov. Lincoln was elected by a close majority. Following is a list of Mayors since Lincoln : Henry Chapin, 1849-50; Peter C. Bacon, 1851-2; John S. C. Knowlton, 1853-4; George W. Richardson, 1855 and 1857; Isaac Davis, 1856, 1858 and 1861; Alexander H. Bullock, 1859; William W. Rice in 1860; P. Emory Aldrich, 1862; D. Waldo Lincoln, 1863-4; Phineas Ball, 1865; James B. Blake, 1866-70; Edward Earle, 1871; George F. Verry, 1872; Clark Jillson, 1873, 1875-6; Edward L. Davis, 1874; Charles B. Pratt, 1877-9; Frank H. Kelley, 1880-1; Elijah B. Stoddard, 1882; and Samuel E. Hildreth, the present [1883] incumbent.

207   **1853.**   Rev. Henry Ward Beecher lectured before the City Anti-Slavery Society.

208   **1873.**   Fanny Janauschek in *Chesney Wold.*

April 9.

209   **1836.**   Citizens Bank incorporated.

210   **1865.**   News of Lee's surrender.

The despatch announcing the event was received late on Sunday evening, and 100 guns were immediately fired on the Common.

April 10.

211   **1796.**   "Sacred to the memory of Major William Treadwell, who died April 10, A. D. 1796, Aet 46.

"He enter'd the army in 1775, and devoted his whole time to the service of his Country, until the Independence of America was secured, he ever courted the field of battle, & his bravery was indesputable.

"A member of Capt. Timothy Bigelow's company of minute men which left Worcester, April 19, 1775. He was 2d lieutenant in Col. Thomas Crafts' regiment of artillery in the same year. About 1783 the Worcester Artillery was formed, and he was chosen captain. He was an original member of the Society of the Cincinnati."—*Inscriptions from the Old Burial Grounds.*

212 **1865.** Celebration of Lee's surrender.

Business was generally suspended. Salutes were fired in different parts of the city. The Fire Department and other organizations paraded. There was a general illumination in the evening.

213 **1873.** Anton Rubinstein, the celebrated pianist and composer, at Mechanics Hall.

He was born in Russia in 1829; and appeared in public when only eight years old. He became a pupil of Villoing at Moscow and Paris; and studied composition under Dehn at Berlin. He was for a time pianist to the Grand-Duchess Helena, and director of the Russian Musical Society. In concert tours through Europe and the United States, he achieved a grand success.

214 **1876.** Worcester Continentals organized.

They first paraded in public at the Centennial Celebration, July 4, 1876.

April 11.

215 **1778.** "On Saturday last arrived in Town, and on Sunday proceeded on his way to Newport, where it is said, he is to be exchanged for the much abused Col. Ethan Allen, Lieut. Col. Campbell of the 71st regiment."—*Spy, Thursday, April 16, 1778.*

April 12.

216 **1773.** "Here lies inter'd the body of Major Daniel Heywood, who departed this life April 12th 1773 in ye 79th year of his age. He was an early settler in this town and one of the first Deacons of the church in this Place, in which office he continued to the day of his Death. This monument is erected at the desire and Expence of his Grandson & Heir, Daniel Heywood.

Psalm 90: 10: His epitaph.

"Was son of Deacon John Heywood of Concord, and came to Worcester in 1718. Married for his first wife Hannah Ward, daughter of Obediah Ward. Was chosen captain of the first military company formed in the town, and town treasurer in 1722. Held the office of Selectman twenty years, between 1724 and 1753, and was Town Clerk in 1753. Was major of a company in his majesty's service that marched to the defence of the western frontier, August 8th, 1748."—*Inscriptions from the Old Burial Grounds.*

April 13.

217   **1731.** "Whearas many Small Children Cannot attend yᵉ Schoole in yᵉ Center of yᵉ Town by Reason of yᵉ remotness of their Dwellings and to yᵉ intent that all Childrin may have yᵉ benefite of Education, &c.

"Voted that a Suitable number of Schoole Dames, not exceeding five, be provided by yᵉ Selectmen at yᵉ Charge of yᵉ Town for yᵉ teaching of Small Childrin to read, and to be placed in yᵉ Several parts of yᵉ Town as yᵉ Selectmen may think most Conveinent, and Such Gentlewomen to be payd by yᵉ pole as yᵉ Selectmen & they may agree."—*Early Records of Worcester.*

218   **1867.** George H. Ward, Post 10, Grand Army of the Republic chartered.

April 14.

219   **1772.** "Here lie buried the remains of Lieut. Luke Brown, who having taken the infection of the small pox at New York and died of the same after his return home, viz: April 14, 1772. Aged 58. Buried here to prevent the spread of the infection.

Luke Brown came to Worcester from Sudbury sometime before 1750, and kept the public house which was burned Christmas eve, 1824, and which stood near the ancient first jail. He acquired wealth by speculating in public lands. It was while on a journey to New York for the purpose of purchasing the town now called Newfane, in Vermont, that he caught the small pox. His body was buried on the north side of the Jo Bill road. Report says that he had few friends, was avaricious, and procured his property not perhaps by the most honorable means.

"In the French war he was lieutenant of a detachment of men from Col. John Chandler's regiment under Capt. John Curtis, that marched to the relief of Fort William Henry in 1759."—*Inscriptions from the Old Burial Grounds.*

220   1820.   Death of Hon. Levi Lincoln, senior.

He was born in Hingham, May 15, 1749. Came to Worcester in 1775; Clerk of the Courts in 1775; and Judge of Probate from 1777 to 1781. He became a member of both branches of the Legislature; and in 1800 was elected to Congress. He was Attorney General of the United States, 1801-5; Lieutenant Governor of Massachusetts, 1807-8; and became Governor in consequence of the death of Gov. Sullivan in 1809. He was the father of a distinguished family.

221   1861.   News of the fall of Fort Sumter.

The anxiously awaited tidings were received on Sunday evening, and great excitement prevailed, Spy extras were disposed of to the crowd as fast as they could be printed for several hours.

April 15.

222   1865.   Death of President Lincoln.

The dispatch announcing the assassination was received about midnight, and the citizens were aroused from their beds by the tolling of bells. News of the President's death was received early in the morning. The City Council met at 7, and after consultation a public meeting was called, which gathered in Mechanics Hall at 10. Hon. A. H. Bullock presided, and the exercises were of a religious character. Stores and dwellings were draped, and manifestations of mourning were general.

223   1869.   First performance in Worcester, of Theodore Thomas's Orchestra.

April 16.

224   1861.   First War Meeting.

In the City Hall, presided over by the Mayor, Hon. Isaac Davis. Addresses were made by distinguished citizens, and "the meeting was unanimous, hearty and enthusiastic."

225   1872.   Memorial observance of the death of Samuel F. B. Morse, inventor of the Telegraph.

In the Council Chamber, City Hall. A sketch of Prof. Morse, written by Rev. George Allen, was read by Col. John D. Washburn.

G

April 17.

226   **1828.** Worcester County Institution for Savings organized.

227   **1848.** First City Government inaugurated.

228   **1861.** Departure of the Worcester Light Infantry for the seat of war.

> The Light Infantry belonged to the Sixth Regiment, but were with the detachment that passed safely through Baltimore at the time of the riot, April 19th, and proceeded directly to Washington. The time of their service was mostly spent in Maryland. They arrived home on the 1st of August.

April 18.

229   **1864.** Departure of the 57th Regiment.

> This regiment participated in the Battle of the Wilderness; spent the summer before Petersburg; and were engaged in numerous minor encounters until the close of the war. It was mustered out in August, 1865.

April 19.

230   **1774.** The Grand Jury refused to serve under Chief Justice Peter Oliver, who was charged with high crimes and misdemeanors by the House of Representatives.

> The Grand Jury presented a remonstrance to the Court; but upon being assured that the Chief Justice would not attend, were sworn and performed their duty.

231   **1775.** 110 men marched from Worcester on the alarm at Lexington.

> "Before noon, on the 19th of April, an express came to the town, shouting, as he passed through the street at full speed, 'to arms! to arms! war is begun!' His white horse, bloody with spurring, and dripping with sweat, fell exhausted near the church. Another was instantly procured, and the tidings went on. The bell rang out the alarm, cannon were fired, and messengers sent to every part of the town to collect the soldiery. . . . . . In a short time the minute men were paraded on the green, under Capt. Timothy Bigelow; after fervent prayer by the Rev. Mr. Maccarty, they took up the line of march. They were soon followed by as many of the train bands as could be gathered, under Capt. Benjamin Flagg."—*Lincoln's History.*

232   **1833.**   Death of Dr. William Paine.

He was the eldest son of Hon. Timothy Paine, born in Worcester, June 5, 1750. Was educated in England; a loyalist in the Revolution; and was appointed Apothecary to the forces in America. After the war he resided in the British Provinces, and on the death of his father, returned to Worcester. "He possessed extensive professional learning and refined literary taste, and was equally respected as a physician and a citizen."

233   **1854.**   Death of Hon. John Davis.

Was born in Northborough, Jan. 13, 1787. Graduated at Yale College in 1812; admitted to the bar in 1815. A Member of Congress from 1825 to 1833; Governor, 1833-5 and 1841-3; and United States Senator, 1835-41, and 1845-53. He was popularly known as "Honest John Davis."

234   **1861.**   Dedication of the monument to Col. Timothy Bigelow, on the Common.

The monument was erected by Timothy Bigelow Lawrence of Boston, a great-grandson of the revolutionary hero. A military and civic procession paraded the streets; a salute was fired; and at the monument addresses were made by T. B. Lawrence, Esq., Mayor Davis, Ex-Gov. Lincoln, Rev. Andrew Bigelow, D. D. and Hon. John P. Bigelow of Boston, (grandsons of Col. Bigelow,) Hon. B. F. Thomas; and the venerable Tyler Bigelow of Watertown, a nephew of Col. Bigelow.

April 20.

235   **1859.**   Hon. Carl Schurz lectured in the City Hall.

236   **1861.**   Departure of the Third Battalion of Rifles.

Made up of the Worcester City Guards, the Emmet Guards, and the Holden Rifles; the battalion commanded by Major Charles Devens. They were on duty about Baltimore most of their time of service, and arrived home on the 2d of August.

April 21.

237   **1830.** $2,500 voted by the Town to purchase land for the State Lunatic Hospital.

238   **1848.**   Mechanics Bank incorporated.

April 23.

239   1865.   Memorial Discourse on Abraham Lincoln by Rev. Seth Sweetser, D. D.

This Discourse was printed.

April 24.

240   1775.   John Hancock and Samuel Adams, delegates to the Continental Congress, arrived in Worcester.

They remained two days waiting for a suitable escort to Philadelphia. A letter written by Hancock at this time, is printed in the "Hundred Boston Orators," page 92.

April 25.

241   1871.   Trinity Methodist Episcopal Church dedicated.

April 26.

242   1845.   Worcester Aqueduct Company organized.

This Company was incorporated Feb. 28, 1845, for the purpose of constructing and maintaining an aqueduct, to conduct water from Bladder Pond for the use of the town.   Stephen Salisbury, Isaac Davis, William A. Wheeler, Henry W. Miller and Samuel Davis were the Committee of Managers.   The right and property of this company were purchased by the city, June 8, 1848.

243   1852.   Visit of Louis Kossuth.

He arrived at 4.30 P. M. from Springfield, and was received with ringing of bells and firing of cannon; flags and decorations were displayed. Kossuth rode in procession to the Common, where he was introduced to the people by Mayor Bacon at the speakers' stand, and made a very eloquent address.   He also addressed a meeting at the City Hall in the evening.

April 27.

244   1861.   An effigy of Jeff. Davis was discovered hanging at the corner of Main & Elm streets.

April 28.

245   **1789.** "On Tuesday last, the first piece of Corduroy made at the manufactory in this town [on School street] was taken from the loom."—*Spy, Thursday, April 30, 1789.*

246   **1846.** Church of the Unity dedicated.

247   **1873.** Gipsies warned to depart the town.

In the ancient times in New England it was the custom upon the appearance of strangers within the town, for the constable to order them to depart forthwith. This salutary method was revived by Mayor Jillson, who proclaimed that "Whereas. it has been customary in years past for large numbers of wandering vagrants, known as 'Gipsies,' to camp in the suburbs of the city, without any visible purpose except 'plunder'; therefore in view of this great annoyance, and the liability that diseases dangerous to public health may break out in some of these camps, they are ordered to forthwith leave the city." This action was criticized as being high-handed and unconstitutional; but the Mayor took the responsibllity, and the Gipsies went.

April 29.

248   **1790.** "Last Thursday in the afternoon, the Hon. *John Jay*, Esq., Chief Justice of the United States, arrived in this Town, and the next morning sat out for Boston." —*Spy, Thursday, May 6, 1790.*

249   **1846.** Rev. Edward Everett Hale ordained Pastor of the Church of the Unity,

He was dismissed July 27, 1856.

250   **1861.** $3000 voted by the City Council to aid enlistments.

To be expended in uniforms and equipments.

April 30.

251   **1814.** Rev. Samuel Austin, D. D. brought suit to recover Ministerial Land sold by the Town.

Judgment was rendered for the demandant, but was released by the Parish.

May 1.

252   1837.   The Town voted to receive its portion of the surplus revenue of the United States.

The first instalment amounted to over $6,000.   Of the whole amount, $7,000 was paid towards the debt of the town, and Main street was paved with part of the remainder.

253   1840.   "HARRISONISM IN WORCESTER.

"Harrisonism exhibited itself in this Town on Friday of last week, in a manner that has inflicted a lasting disgrace upon the party.   It was expected that a large number of delegates to the Whig Convention at Baltimore would pass through town that afternoon ; and accordingly certain prominent men of the Harrison party made preparation to give them a welcome, after the established form in which Harrisonism now exhibits its hospitality.   They took a barrel of *hard cider*, highly charged, it is said, with *brandy*, and mounted it conspicuously in the Depot building of the Boston & Worcester Railroad.   A pole was stuck into the bunghole, across the top of which was a signboard bearing the conspicuous inscription — 'HARD CIDER ; *Help Yourselves.*'   And underneath was hung a miserable mockery of our national flag—a Harrison pocket handkerchief.   Hard crackers and cheese flanked the sides of the barrel, and a noisy dandy negro officiated as master of ceremonies.   The cars having been delayed on the road two hours beyond their time, and the cider having circulated freely in the meantime, among the devotees, old and young, of the 'hard cider candidate,' the 'Harrison enthusiasm' had got to so high a pitch when the cars came in that it burst forth as though Pandemonium had let loose its masses.   Prominent Whigs were screaming 'hard cider' at the top of their voices ; pails of it were thrust into the cars, along with broken cheese and baskets of crackers, where it was caught up by Whig dandies in kid gloves, with as much apparent delight as the caged beasts in a menagerie seize their daily allowance of refuse meat."—*Worcester Palladium, Wednesday, May 6, 1840.*

254   1844.   Quinsigamond Lodge, No. 43, Independent Order of Odd Fellows instituted.

The first Lodge chartered in Worcester. Other Lodges are Worcester, No. 56; Central, No. 168, formed Sept. 17, 1874; and Ridgely, No. 112.

255   1861.   Home Guards organized.

Consisting of the honorary and past members, and the friends of the Worcester Light Infantry. The officers were: Captain, D. Waldo Lincoln; First Lieut., Henry W. Conklin; Second Lieut., W. A. Williams; Third Lieut., Putnam W. Taft; Fourth Lieut., Ivers Phillips; Clerk, R. M. Gould. This company was composed mostly of elderly men, and performed escort duty, attended soldiers' funerals, etc., until replaced by the State Guards in 1863.

May 2.

256   1818.   Death of William Charles White.

Actor, dramatist, and lawyer, born in Boston in 1777. He appeared at the Federal Street Theatre, Boston, in 1796, as *Norval*. He wrote "Orlando," a tragedy, some minor poems and plays, and two or three novels. In 1801, he left the stage, and turned his attention to the law. Removed to Worcester where he edited the *National Ægis* for a time; and in 1811, was appointed County Attorney. He published a Compendium of the Laws of Massachusetts in 3 vols., and two orations.

257   1825.   Town Hall dedicated.

An address was delivered by Hon. John Davis. The cost of the building was about $10,000. It has been enlarged and several times remodeled.

May 3.

258   1850.   Explosion in the Mayor's office.

An attempt was made about midnight to blow up the building on Main street, near Sudbury, in which was the office of Mayor Chapin, by means of a 6 inch hand grenade. The concussion was very severe; the door of the office was broken to fragments, and a piece of the shell went through the brick wall in the rear, while the building was considerably shattered. This outrage was one result of the temperance agitation, in which Mayor Chapin had taken a prominent part; and the principal in the affair was Jubal Harrington, quondam Postmaster, and editor of the *Republican*, who had promised to give the Free Soilers and Temperance

Agitators "hell and scissors." Harrington forfeited his bonds and fled to California, where he became a judge and a man of consequence.

259   **1775.** First issue of *The Massachusetts Spy* in Worcester. The Spy was issued from the press in Worcester after a suspension of three weeks, during which time Mr. Thomas, with the aid of General Joseph Warren and Colonel Timothy Bigelow, effected the removal of his establishment from Boston. This number contains an account of the Battle of Lexington, in which the publisher took part. The first impression is in possession of the American Antiquarian Society, and bears Mr. Thomas's certificate that it was the first thing ever printed in Worcester.

260   **1811.** "On Friday last, *Caleb Jephterson* was exposed in this town in the Pillory, for one hour and an half, pursuant to his sentence, upon three several convictions, for the odious and detestable crime of Blasphemy."—*Spy, Wednesday, May 8, 1811.*

May 4.

261   **1750.** [From the Warrant for a Town Meeting, May 4th, 1750: "For yᵉ Town to Come into Some method that People may Sit in yᵉ Seats [in the meeting house] assigned to prevent Disorders & that they dont put themselves too forward."]
"Voted that yᵉ late Seators give Tickitts to Such People who have not taken their Seats properly according to yᵉ Last Seating directing them to Sit whear they ought to prevent Disorder and fill up properly any Pews latley built according to yᵉ Design of yᵉ Town in making the Grants."—*Early Records.*

May 5.

262   **1779.** Lemuel Burnham and Joshua Mossman were publicly whipped forty stripes each, for passing counterfeit money.

May 6.

263   **1657.** The first grant of land in the vicinity of Worcester was made by the General Court of Massachusetts to Increase Nowell of Charlestown, and comprised 3,200 acres.

264 **1844.** Convention of those opposed to the annexation of Texas.

At the Town Hall. Hon. Solomon Strong of Leominster was president. Resolutions condemnatory of the course of the administration were adopted. Hon. Charles Allen made an address; and additional resolutions were offered by Rev. George Allen.

May 7.

265 **1872.** Rum Sellers celebrate their victory by a street parade.

On the question "Shall any person be allowed to manufacture, sell, or keep for sale, ale, porter, strong beer, or lager beer in this city," the vote stood, yes, 2143; no, 2115. In the evening, all the liquor shops closed doors at an early hour. A band of music in a wagon followed by a large and noisy crowd, went through some of the principal streets. Bonfires were kindled in different parts of the city, and some riotous conduct was manifested.

May 9.

266 **1775.** "May 10.—The commanding officer at Cambridge has given leave to the regulars who were taken prisoners, either to go to Boston and join their respective regiments, or have liberty to work in the country for those who will employ them. In consequence of which, those who were confined in Worcester, Massachusetts, fifteen in number, heartily requested to be employed by the people, not choosing to return to their regiments to fight against their American brethren, though some of them expressed their willingness to spill their blood in defence of their King in a righteous cause. They all set out yesterday for different towns."—*Pennsylvania Journal, May 24, 1775.*

267 **1862.** Anna E. Dickinson lectured in Washburn Hall.

Her first appearance in Worcester.

268 **1873.** Home for Aged Females dedicated.

H

May 10.

269   **1828.** The Town voted to purchase the Pine Meadow Burial Ground.

This lot comprising eight acres was bought of Samuel Hathaway for $100 per acre. No interments were made here of late years; and since 1870, all the bodies have been removed to other places.

May 11.

270   **1801.** Oliver Ellsworth passed through Worcester on his return from France.

Ellsworth was prominent in the revolutionary councils of Connecticut, and a member of the Convention for framing the Constitution of the United States. He served as Senator from 1789 to 1795, when he was appointed Chief Justice by President Washington. In 1799, he was associated with William R. Davie and William Vans Murray, to adjust the differences with France. He was born in 1745, and died in 1807.

271   **1829.** Death of Stephen Salisbury, senior.

He came to Worcester from Boston before the Revolution, and opened a store just north of Lincoln square, in the ownership of which his brother Samuel, who carried on the business in Boston, was concerned. The Salisbury mansion, at the head of Main street, was erected by them.

May 12.

272   **1842.** Car manufactory of Bradley and Rice burned.

At Washington square. Loss, $20,000.

273   **1860.** Reception to Hon. Isaac Davis, on his return from the Charleston Convention.

Col. Davis was a delegate to the National Democratic Convention at Charleston, South Carolina; and was firm in his allegiance to Stephen A. Douglas. On his arrival home he was received at Washington sqr. by the Worcester Light Infantry and National Band, with a large body of citizens, and escorted to his residence, where he was addressed by George W. Bentley and made an appropriate reply.

May 13.

274   **1726.** "Voted that Thanks be returned to ye Hon^rbl Adam winthrop, Esqr. for his bounty in bestowing a Cushing on y^e

Town as furniture for ye pulpit. , and that ye Town Clerk present his Honr. a Coppy of S^d vote."—*Early Records.*

275   **1856.**   Edward Everett delivered his Oration on Washington, in the City Hall.

"After the sectional warfare of opinion and feeling reached a dangerous height, anxious if possible to bring a counteractive and conciliating influence into play, ... I devoted the greater part of my time for three years to the attempt to give new strength in the hearts of my countrymen to the last patriotic feeling in which they seemed to beat in entire unison,—veneration and love for the name of Washington, and reverence for the place of his rest.   With this object in view, I travelled thousands of miles, by night and by day, in midwinter and midsummer, speaking three, four, and five times a week, in feeble health, and under a heavy burden of domestic care and sorrow, and inculcating the priceless value of the Union in precisely the same terms from Maine to Georgia and from New York to St. Louis."—*Public Speech of Mr. Everett.*

The Mount Vernon Fund, collected through the efforts of Mr. Everett and which was applied to the purchase of Washington's home estate, amounted to nearly $100,000.

276   **1864.**   People's Savings Bank incorporated.

277   **1879.**   August Wilhelmj, the renowned violinist, at Mechanics Hall.

May 14.

278   **1872.**   Deacon Benjamin Butman died, aged 85.

He was a native of Worcester, and began mercantile life in 1808 as a clerk in the drug store of George Brinley, in Boston.   He commenced business in Worcester in 1816 or 17 as a dealer in West India goods. He retired in 1836; built Butman, Brinley and Warren blocks; and became a heavy real estate owner.   President of the Central Bank, 1829-36; also president of the Citizens' Bank.   About 1812, he purchased 45 acres of land bounded by Main, Pleasant, Newbury and Chandler streets, for which he paid $7,000.

May 15.

279   **1667.**   Capt. Daniel Gookin, Capt. Edward Johnson, Samuel Andrew and Andrew Belcher, were ordered by the Gen-

eral Court to take an exact view of "a place about 10 miles westward of Marlborrow called Quandsicamond ponds," and to make report "whether it be capable to make a village," etc.

In their report the committee stated: "Wee conceue therre may bee enough medow forr a small plantation orr towne of about thirrty families," and if certain former grants were annexed, "it, may supply about sixty families."

280   1851.   Mechanics Savings Bank incorporated.

281   1851.   Ralph Waldo Emerson lectured on the Fugitive Slave Law.

282   1861.   Charlotte Cushman as *Meg Merrilies*, at the theatre.
Miss Cushman died Feb. 18, 1876, in her 60th year.

May 16.

283   1791.   Two shocks of an earthquake in this and neighboring towns.

284   1832.   In the SPY of this date the selectmen are criticized for licensing "a company of strolling actors calling themselves Circus Riders, to exhibit their fooleries here"; and it further says: "Who does not know that no one gets any good by attending such exhibitions?—That by going there he encourages idleness, cruelty and vice? It is hoped that this is the last time we shall be troubled with such unwelcome visitors."

285   1874.   Col. James Estabrook died, aged 77.
He was born in Holden, and came to Worcester in 1829, when he engaged in the grocery business with Gen. Nathan Heard at the old "Green Store," on Main street, nearly opposite the Court House. Subsequently he was in business in Boston. He was an Alderman of Worcester in 1848-9; and Sheriff of the County, 1851-2. He possessed large wealth, the result of careful investments in real estate.

May 17.

286   1806.   "ERECTED in memory of MR. LEMUEL RICE Æt. 66. and MR. LUKE RICE Æt. 62. who died within 15 minutes of each other on May 17, 1806. Brothers which were united in life and not divided in death.

"Lemuel Rice was private in Capt. David Chadwick's company that marched to Hadley, Aug. 28, 1777. Jailor from 1788 to 98. His daughter married Benjamin Russell, editor of the Boston *Columbian Centinel.*"—*Inscriptions from the Old Burial Grounds.*

May 18.

287 1767. Instructions to Joshua Bigelow, senior, Representative to the General Court: "That you use your Influence to obtain a law to put an End to that unchristian and Impolitick Practice of making Slaves of the Humane Speices in this Province and that you give your vote for none to serve in his Majestys Council who you may have Reason to think will use their Influence against such a Law or that Sustain any office Incompatible with such Trust and in such Choice Prefer such Gentleman only who have Distinguished themselves in the Defence of our Liberty."— *Worcester Town Records.*

288 1773. Declaration of Rights approved.

This Declaration is printed in the Collections of The Worcester Society of Antiquity, Vol. IV., page 203.

289 1854. J. S. Orr, alias "Angel Gabriel," with his brazen trumpet, collected a crowd, and began the delivery of a "No Popery" harangue, when he was arrested by the police for disturbing the peace, and locked up. A large and excited crowd gathered about the Common, where Dexter F. Parker made a speech "full of sound and fury," as the Spy has it; followed by others. The assemblage soon became violent: stones were thrown, one hitting Sheriff George, W. Richardson on the head; and a rescue of the prisoner was threatened. Finally, the City Guards were ordered out, and the rioters dispersed.

"Gabriel" was a Scotchman, Sandy McSwish by name, although he called himself Orr or Horr. His father was of the Clan Gordon. Sandy was born on the Isle of Skye, Sept. 3, 1809. He was bound apprentice to a weaver. His father having died, his mother married a Baptist minister named Orr. Sandy joined a company of strolling players; afterwards was a Methodist preacher; and then came to America and joined the Mormons. After following various avocations, he finally

began preaching in public places against popish authority and foreign
influence. He had a horn or trumpet which he blew to attract an
audience, hence the name "Gabriel." He acted as an adjunct to the
Native American or "Know Nothing" party, which performed a praise-
worthy service in annihilating the old Whig party.

May 19.

290   1783.   Protest against the return of the absentees or tories.

Printed in the Collections of The Worcester Society of Antiquity, Vol.
IV., pp. 440-444.

291   1877.   Hon. Edward Earle died, aged 67.

He was born in Leicester; came to Worcester in 1832, and opened a
store for the sale of flour, on Central street. Afterwards was in the
iron trade with Joseph Pratt, from which he retired in 1848, when he
sold his interest to F. H. Inman. He then engaged in the card cloth-
ing business with his half-brother, Timothy K. Earle, from which he
withdrew a few years before his death. Mr. Earle was chosen Selectman, Representative and Alderman; and in 1871, was elected Mayor
to serve the unexpired term of James G. Blake. He was a prominent
member of the Society of Friends.

292   1878.   [Sunday] D. L. Moody, the celebrated Evangelist,
preached afternoon and evening in Mechanics Hall.

May 20.

293   1724.   First allotment of pews in the meeting house.

See Early Records of Worcester, Book I., pp. 24-26.

294   1852.   Worcester Musical Association formed.

This organization had no connection with the present Worcester County
Musical Association. It existed about three years.

295   1861.   Dispatches in the Telegraph Office seized by government officials.

Simultaneous action took place throughout the northern states, and
considerable treason was brought to light.

296   1873.   A house on Millstone hill was taken by the sheriff,
by virtue of a warrant from two justices of the peace, to be
used as a hospital for small pox patients.

Considerable opposition to this action was manifested in the Board of Aldermen, some claiming that Mayor Jillson had overstepped his authority in seizing private property; but on the testimony of prominent physicians that the exigencies of the case necessitated prompt measures, he was sustained. At this time there were 75 cases of small pox in the city, knowledge of which was kept from the public. Happily, the malady quickly subsided, and the building was not used.

May 21.

297   1777.   "Here lyes interr'd the remains of Capt. Daniel Ward, who departed this life May 21st 1777, in the 77th year of his age."—*Inscriptions from the Old Burial Grounds.*

Was son of Obediah Ward, an original settler of Worcester. Daniel built a house opposite the Common, which he sold in 1750 to Sheriff Gardner Chandler, who erected on the spot the fine mansion, occupied later by Judge Barton, and which was removed to make way for Taylor's Building.

298   1836.   First Baptist Church burned.

On the site of the present edifice, east of the Common. This church was erected in 1813. The fire was the act of an incendiary.

299   1874.   Death of John P. Kettell.

He was born in Boston in 1797; came to Worcester in 1818, and opened a shop in Lincoln square for the manufacture and sale of hats, caps, furs, etc., in which business he continued until his death. He occupied successively stores in Goddard's Row, Butman Block, and Universalist Church building, corner of Main and Foster streets. He was one of the founders of the Mechanics Association, Selectman, and Deacon of the First Unitarian Church.

300   1878.   First National Dog Show, in Mechanics Hall.

May 22.

301   1801.   Lightning struck the house of Judge Edward Bangs, on the east side of Main street, opposite the Court House, doing considerable damage to the wood work, and breaking two large looking glasses.

302   1821.   Rev. Arætius B. Hull ordained Pastor of the Old South Church.

Mr. Hull died in Worcester, May 17, 1826.

303   1852.   Hope Cemetery consecrated.

The City Council and a large concourse of citizens were present. Mayor Bacon made a short address, detailing the reasons for the purchase of the ground. Prayer was offered by Rev. E. E. Hale, and Rev. Elam Smalley delivered an address. The exercises closed with prayer by Rev. S. Sweetser, and singing by the choir.

Hope Cemetery originally comprised 50 acres, and was purchased in 1851 for $1,855. Additions have been made to the original tract.

May 23.

304   1776.   "The Town voted unanimously that if the Continental Congress should declare the American Colonies independent of Great Britain that they will support the measure with their lives and fortunes."—*Worcester Town Records.*

May 24.

305   1856.   Indignation Meeting in consequence of the assault on Senator Sumner.

At the City Hall. J. S. C. Knowlton presided; and speeches were made by P. Emory Aldrich, Dr. Cutler, Judge Allen, Dexter F. Parker, J. B. D. Cogswell and Rev. Horace James. Resolutions severely condemning the outrage were adopted.

May 25.

306   1767.   Dwelling house of James Barber burned.

307   1861.   First New Hampshire Regiment passed through the city, bound for the seat of war.

It was received by local military companies and escorted to Mechanics Hall, where a welcome was extended by Mayor Davis, and a collation served.

May 26.

308   1876.   Samuel J. Frost executed.

For the murder of his brother-in-law at Petersham the previous July. When the drop fell, the force of the fall was so great that the rope cut nearly through the neck, almost severing the head from the body.

May 27.

309   **1845.** Laying of the corner stone of St. John's Church, Temple street.

310   **1854.** Indignation Meeting in consequence of the seizure in Boston of Anthony Burns, an escaped slave.

At the City Hall. Speeches were made by W. W. Rice, Dr. O. Martin, Thomas Drew, T. W. Higginson and S. S. Foster. It was "voted unanimously to lay aside business Monday, [this meeting was on Saturday evening] and proceed to Boston *en masse* to meet the friends of liberty . . . . . to take counsel upon the emergencies of the times." 900 persons went to Boston on the 27th; and on Monday the 29th, there was a special train with tickets at half-price, of which a large number availed themselves.

May 28.

311   **1791.** "Saturday night last, Stephen Burroughs, Stephen Cook, Stephen Cook, Jun. and Simon Wetherbee, who were confined in the gaol in this town, effected their escape by sawing a passage for themselves through the grates. . . . . . One hour in the pillory, thirty stripes, and about seven weeks imprisonment were yet due to Burroughs."—*Spy, Thursday, June 2, 1791.*

Burroughs had, for immoralities committed, as was alleged, in Charlton where he was teaching school, been sentenced to receive one hundred and seventeen stripes on the naked back; to stand two hours in the pillory; to sit one hour on the gallows with a rope around his neck; to remain confined in prison three months; and procure bonds for his good behavior for seven years. His conviction appears to have been unwarranted by the evidence, which was questionable and slender, while the sentence imposed by the judges, whose minds were evidently biased by the former reputation of the prisoner, was unreasonably severe and out of proportion to the offence. There is some evidence to show that the public sympathy in his behalf, openly expressed, was finally manifested in a practical manner. In the published memoirs of Burroughs, the statement is made "that many people in the vicinity were of opinion that he was too severely punished, among whom were some of the first characters in the county. Burroughs was aware of this, and cherished secret hopes of deliverance. One night about 12 o'clock, he says

I

his prison door was forced open, and he was requested to depart. He walked out, and passed between two ranks of people to a great distance; the number appearing to him not less than a thousand. All this time there was a profound silence; and he departed, ignorant of the names of his deliverers."

312   1833.   Exhibition of the Blind by Dr. S. G. Howe.

In the Old South Church. A collection was taken which amounted to $200.

313   1875.   Taylor's Building burned.

On Main street, opposite the Common. This building was erected on the site of the Gardner Chandler mansion by R. C. Taylor in 1870, at a cost of $160,000. The fire began at sunset and burned fiercely until midnight, being confined mostly to the upper stories. In the pecuniary loss, this conflagration was exceeded, of those which have occurred in Worcester, only by the Merrifield fire of 1854.

May 29.

314   1868.   Ex-Governor Levi Lincoln died, aged 85.

He was born in Worcester, Oct. 25, 1782. Graduated at Harvard College in 1802, and was admitted to the bar in 1805. State Senator, 1812; Representative, 1816-23; Speaker, 1822; Lieut.-Governor, 1823; Judge of Supreme Court, 1824; Governor, 1825-34; Member of Congress, 1835-41; Collector of Boston, 1841 to Sept. 1843; State Senator, 1844-45; President of the Senate, 1845; and first Mayor of Worcester, 1848.

May 30.

315   1868.   First observance of Memorial or Decoration Day by the Grand Army.

May 31.

316   1812.   [Sunday] Ordinance of Baptism by Immersion first administered in Worcester.

317   1813.   "In Memory of Dea^n John Chamberlain who died May 31, 1813. Æt. 68.

"Dea. John Chamberlain was the eldest son of Dea. Jacob Chamberlain. Was disarmed by the Committee of Correspondence in May, 1775. Selectman from 1785 to 1802, three years excepted. Was Deacon of the First Parish twenty-two years from 1791 to 1812. He married Mary, daughter of Capt. John Curtis; and his son, Hon. John Curtis Chamberlain, was a distinguished lawyer of Charlestown N. H., and a Member of Congress from that state. Another son, Gen. Thomas Chamberlain, was Crier of the Courts for seventeen years previous to his death, and was the first President of the Common Council of the city of Worcester. He filled most of the military offices from corporal to brigadier general with the highest honor to himself, and to the satisfaction of his command. Another son, Levi, a lawyer of distinction at Fitzwilliam, N. H., afterwards at Keene, where he died, was a member of the Peace Congress. Another son, Henry, was also a lawyer, who practised law in Maine and Georgia."—*Inscriptions from the Old Burial Grounds.*

June 1.

318   1865.   Eulogy on Abraham Lincoln by Alexander H. Bullock.

Delivered in Mechanics Hall before the City Government and citizens of Worcester. The Eulogy was printed by order of the City Council.

319   1872.   Edward A. Sothern as *Lord Dundreary*, at the Theatre.

320   1881.   Rev. Roland A. Wood installed Pastor of the Church of the Unity.

The sermon was preached by the Rev. Dr. H. W. Bellows of N. Y.

321   1883.   Mrs. Langtry, the *Jersey Lily*, at the Theatre.

The play was Gilbert's comedy of *Pygmalion and Galatea;* and the prices of admission were $1,00, $1,50 and $2,00. The audience was not a large one.

June 2.

322   1776.   "Here lies Buried the Body of Capt. James Goodwin, who departed this life June 2nd 1776, in y^e 62^d year of his age.

"Capt. James Goodwin was captain of a company of men under Col. John Chandler, which left Worcester on the alarm for the relief of Fort William Henry in 1757. In 1760 he was captain of a company of militia numbering forty-eight men. Selectman, 1759. A signer of the royalist protest of 1774."—*Inscriptions from the Old Burial Grounds.*

323   1854.   Business suspended in consequence of the rendition of Anthony Burns.

Stores were closed and draped in mourning; bells were tolled; and flags displayed reversed and at half-mast. A meeting was held on the Common, and adressed by W. W. Rice, Rev. Mr. Adams, Dexter F. Parker and Adin Thayer.

324   **1856.**   Lincoln House opened.

The rear portion of this block was erected by Hon. Levi Lincoln, about 1812, and occupied by him as a residence until 1835, when it became the "Worcester House." In 1843, James H. Wall and Edward H. Hemenway purchased the property, which comprised 33,000 sqr. ft. of land, for $14,000, and erected a one-story building in front, divided into seven stores known as the "tombs." These were removed in 1854 and the present Lincoln House Block erected, to which the old building in the rear was joined. The front portion has not been used as a hotel for nearly twenty years.

325   **1874.**   Worcester Firemen's Relief Association organized.

June 3.

326   **1841.**   Universalist Society formed.

327   **1862.**   Gottschalk, the celebrated pianist, at Washburn Hall.

Louis Moreau Gottschalk was born at New Orleans in 1829, and died at Rio de Janeiro in 1869. He was educated in Paris; and made his first appearance in Europe. He returned to America in 1853, where his performances were attended with great success. "His touch combined extreme delicacy with force and dash; and his style of playing had a dreamy and sensuous charm." He composed more than fifty pieces for the piano.

June 4.

328   **1834.**   Worcester Academy or Manual Labor High School dedicated.

329   **1854.**   [Sunday morning] Four Effigies of parties concerned in the rendition of Anthony Burns, were discovered hanging on the Common.

They were labeled as follows: 1. "Pontius Pilate Loring, the Unjust Judge." 2. "Ben Hallet, the Kidnapper." 3. "Caleb Cushing, the Bloodhound." 4. Franklin Pierce, Satan's Journeyman."

June 5.

330   1877. Inspection and acceptance of the new Lynde Brook Dam.

June 6.

331   1804. First public parade of the Worcester Light Infantry, Capt. Levi Thaxter.

332   1876. Anna E. Dickinson as *Anne Boleyn*, in her play "A Crown of Thorns," at the Theatre.

June 7.

333   1812. [Sunday] Rev. Dr. Austin preached two sermons against the Baptists, who were getting a foothold in the town.

"In the first of these two sermons the Baptists were called 'a sneaking set who hovered about the suburbs, not daring to come into the center of the town,' in allusion to their meeting in outer district school houses. In the other discourse, (records Dea. Wilson) 'the Rev. Dr. railed against what he was pleased to denominate the audacity of the Baptists in approaching the droppings of his sanctuary,' alluding to their holding a meeting on the Common."—*Wall's Reminiscences.*

334   1827. Rev. Rodney A. Miller ordained Pastor of the Old South Church.

He was dismissed April 12, 1844. This was Mr. Miller's only pastorate. He died at Troy, N. Y., Sept. 29, 1876, aged 79.

335   1861. Funeral honors to Stephen A. Douglas.

Business was suspended from 10 to 11 A. M.; bells were tolled, and flags displayed at half-mast.

June 8.

336   1782. Grievances enumerated in instructions to the Representative to the General Court.

Printed in the Collections of The Worcester Society of Antiquity, Vol. IV., pp. 423-4.

337   1864. Webster Park dedicated.

A pleasure ground opened at New Worcester for the purpose of increasing travel over the horse railroad. Tame bears and other animals were among the attractions. The Park was closed after a few years.

June 9.

338 **1862.** William G. Brownlow, the noted Tennessee refugee, addressed a meeting in Mechanics Hall.

Parson Brownlow died April 30, 1877, in his 72d year.

June 10.

339 **1747.** Rev. Thaddeus Maccarty installed Pastor of the Church.

340 **1866.** Henry T. Weikle shot.

While arresting a drunken man the officers were set upon by a mob which followed them to the City Hall. A thousand or more gathered about the Police Office, throwing stones and indulging in other violent conduct. An officer named Lowell, on being hit by a missile, fired his revolver into the crowd, fatally wounding Weikle, an inoffensive German, who had been attracted by the disturbance. Lowell was tried, and sentenced to imprisonment for one year. The widow of Weikle was paid $1000 by vote of the City Council.

341 **1879.** Tornado on Main street.

Most of the force was manifested near the Central Church. Trees were broken, chimneys blown down, a building demolished, and two or three roofs torn off.

June 11.

342 **1793.** Morning Star Lodge of Free and Accepted Masons consecrated.

By Most Worshipful Grand Master John Cutter and officers of the Grand Lodge of Massachusetts. A procession marched from Masons' Hall to the North Meeting House, where a sermon was preached by the Rev. Aaron Bancroft.

This Lodge was chartered March 11, 1793, and was the first one in Worcester. The charter members were Nathaniel Paine, Nathaniel Chandler, John Stanton, Ephraim Mower, Clark Chandler, Samuel Chandler, Charles Chandler, Benjamin Andrews, Joseph Torrey, John White, Samuel Brazer, John Stowers and Samuel Flagg. Isaiah Thomas was the first master.

Other Lodges have been chartered as follows: Montacute, June 9, 1859; Athelstan, June 13, 1866; Quinsigamond, Sept. 13, 1871.

343   1871.   Death of John S. C. Knowlton.

He was born at Hopkinton, N. H., in December, 1798. A graduate of Dartmouth College. He established the *Worcester Palladium* in 1834, of which he was editor until his death. State Senator, 1852-3; Mayor of Worcester, 1853-4; and Sheriff of the County, 1857 to 1871.

June 12.

344   1751.   "Here lies Buried the Body of Capt. Benjamin Flagg, Esq who died June 12th 1751, in the 61st year of his age.

"Benjamin Flagg was Selectman of the town for many years; Sheriff of the County from 1743 to 1751; also Representative to the General Court. He was a son of Benjamin Flagg who came from Watertown to Worcester."—*Inscriptions from the Old Burial Grounds.*

345   1845.   Ex-President Martin Van Buren, accompanied by one of his sons, arrived in town and remained at the American House over night.

He was visited by many citizens. Mr. Van Buren was again in Worcester on the 18th of June, 1858.

346   1879.   Polly Stearns Tucker died, aged 82.

Familiarly known as "Aunt Polly Tucker." She was eccentric and unsociable; and for the last twenty-five years of her life, lived with no company except her numerous family of cats. Her house stood on a little triangular piece of land at the corner of Belmont and Plantation streets. She was a daughter of Daniel Stearns.

June 13.

347   1800.   "On Tuesday the 10th inst. Gen. Alexander Hamilton, and his suit arrived at Oxford, to settle the business relative to the discharge of the troops stationed there ; and on Friday last he passed through this town on his way to Boston."—*Spy, June 18, 1800.*

June 14.

348   1722.   Worcester incorporated a town.

349   1848.   Salem Street Church organized.

350   1854. Merrifield's Buildings burned.

On Union, Exchange and Cypress streets. A large number of manu-
facturing establishments were destroyed, and nearly 1000 men thrown
out of employment. The loss was $500,000.

351   1864. Young Men's Christian Association formed.

June 15.

352   1825. Second visit of Lafayette.

He arrived at 2 A. M. and departed at 8 A. M., on his way to Boston to
take part in the ceremony of laying the corner stone of Bunker Hill
Monument. For notice of his first visit to Worcester, see under date
September 3.

353   1870. The Cardiff Giant exhibited in Worcester.

This stone humbug was manufactured from a block of Iowa gypsum in
a stone-cutter's shop in Chicago, and taken to Cardiff, N. Y. and buried.
After a year it was unearthed and placed on exhibition. Eminent
scientists and archæologists were deceived, pronouncing it of great antiquity, and one of the most important discoveries of the age. Its true
character was, however, soon exposed. The originators of this ingen-
ious imposition sold a three-fourths interest in the image for $30,000,
besides making a large sum by its exhibition.

June 16.

354   1777. "The Selectmen presented a list of the names of
persons whom they Esteemed Enemies to this and the other
United States of america. . . . . . The list of their Names is
as follows viz Nahum Willard, David Moore, Samuel Moore,
Cornelius Stowell, Jacob Chamberlain, John Curtis, Gardner
Chandler, Micah Johnson, Joshua Johnson, William Curtis,
Nathan Patch, Joseph Blair, John Barnerd, Palmer Goulding,
Jacob Stevens, Joseph Clark & James Hart Junr."—*Worces-
ter Town Records.*

355   1791. "Sacred to the Memory of M^r. Jonathan Rice, who
died June ye 16th 1791 in the 56th year of his age.

Selectman, 1780. A member of the Committee of Correspondence,
1778-9. A member of the American Political Society. Was one of a
committee appointed by the court to offer the agreement or covenant

for the non-consumption of British goods to the people for signature. He was voted by the town £2, 12s., 10d. for his trouble and expense in secretly conveying, with the assistance of others, four cannon purchased by the town, out of Boston in 1772. He was a deputy sheriff, and went on the night of the second of February, 1787, with 20 horsemen and 150 infantry, to capture or disperse a body of Shays's insurgents who had assembled at New Braintree. The rebels were found posted behind a stone wall, and in the charge upon them, Sheriff Rice was shot through the arm and hand.

356   **1858.**   Reception of the Boston Light Infantry.

By the Worcester City Guards. They were reviewed by Mayor Davis at the City Hall. A street parade followed.

June 17.

357   **1840.**   Great Harrison Celebration.

A salute was fired in the morning. A log cabin 100 by 50 feet had been erected on Salisbury street in which the Whig state convention was held during the forenoon, and John Davis and George Hull were nominated for governor and lieutenant governor. A procession numbering 10,000, comprising delegations from all parts of the state, formed on the Common and marched to the cabin, where speeches were made by distinguished characters. See the Spy of June 24th.

358   **1863.**   State Guards formed.

Ivers Phillips was captain; Dana H. Fitch, first lieutenant; and John R. Green, second lieutenant. This company succeeded the Home Guards. For a history of its organization and services, and the names of those enrolled, see Rev. A. P. Marvin's History of Worcester in the War of the Rebellion, pp. 430-449. The last public appearance of the State Guards was at the dedication of the Soldiers' Monument, July 15, 1874.

359   **1863.**   Gen. John C. Frémont in Worcester.

360   **1869.**   Visit of President Grant.

The President arrived at the Lincoln square station from Groton, where he had been the guest of Secretary of the Treasury, George S. Boutwell. A military and civic procession escorted him through the principal streets to the Bay State House, where dinner was served. Gen. Grant left for New York late in the afternoon.

361   **1871.**   Fire Alarm Telegraph first operated.

J

June 19.

362   1783.   William Huggins and John Mansfield executed for burglary.

363   1841.   [Saturday] Gov. William H. Seward of New York arrived in town, and remained at the Worcester House over Sunday.

June 20.

364   1774.   Tory Protest rejected.

The Loyalists of the town offered a protest against the instructions given the Representative, which severely criticized the attitude of the British Government, and required him to oppose, by his vote, payment for the tea destroyed at Boston.   The protest was published in Boston papers; and Clark Chandler, the Town Clerk, recorded it in the town book.   This entry he was forced to expunge in open meeting.   See under date Aug. 24.   The instructions, protest, and proceedings are printed in the fourth volume of the Collections of the Worcester Society of Antiquity.

June 21.

365   1843.   Corner Stone of Holy Cross College laid.

366   1843.   President John Tyler and Suite passed through Worcester, on their return from the Bunker Hill celebration.

A few hundred persons, who hastily gathered at the station, were gratified with a sight of the Chief Magistrate.   It was not generally known that the President would stop in Worcester.

367   1848.   Free Soil Meeting.

In the City Hall.   Albert Tolman was Chairman, and William A. Wallace, Secretary.   Hon. Charles Allen made a speech in vindication of his action in repudiating the nomination of Zachary Taylor at the Philadelphia Convention.   Henry Wilson, of Natick, also made a brief address.   At the close of the meeting, Rev. George Allen offered the following resolution, which excited great enthusiasm, and was afterwards adopted by Free Soil meetings throughout the state.

"Resolved, that Massachusetts wears no chains, and spurns all bribes; that Massachusetts goes now, and will ever go, for free soil and free men, for free lips and a free press, for a free land and a free world."

June 22.

368   1849. Worcester Gas Light Company formed.

369   1867. President Andrew Johnson and suite passed through Worcester to Boston.

June 23.

370   1845. First Daily Paper.

The DAILY TRANSCRIPT was the first daily paper in Worcester. Julius L. Clarke, subsequently State Auditor and Insurance Commissioner, was editor. The Transcript was purchased by John Milton Earle, May 1, 1847, and incorporated with the "Daily Spy"; the consolidation being continued for a year as the "Transcript," when the name "Daily Spy" was resumed.

June 24.

371   1772. First Stage from Boston to New York passed through Worcester.

372   1848. Mass Meeting to ratify the nominations of Taylor and Fillmore.

Hon. Ira M. Barton was Chairman, and J. C. B. Davis, Secretary. Gov. Lincoln announced that he should, at some future time, reply to the charges made against himself and Gov. Davis by Judge Allen, in his speech of the 21st. Gen. Leslie Combs of Kentucky then addressed the meeting in defense of the Whig nominations.

373   1878. Removal of the Remains of Isaiah Thomas from the Mechanic Street Burial Ground to Rural Cemetery.

The City Government, the Masonic fraternities, and the American Antiquarian Society took part in the dedication of the removed tomb. At Mechanics Hall addresses were made by Mayor Pratt, Hon. Stephen Salisbury, Hon. John D. Baldwin, Hon. H. O. Houghton, Hon. Marshall P. Wilder and Hon. Charles W. Slack; "after which the assembly, with the escort of many Masonic fraternities, followed the remains of Dr. Thomas to the Rural Cemetery, where the re-interment was made with solemn masonic rites, and a graceful eulogy was spoken by M. W. Grand Master, Charles A. Welch."

374   **1878.** Edison's Phonograph or Talking Machine exhibited.

June 25.

375   **1860.** A salute of 100 guns was fired in honor of the nomination of Stephen A. Douglas for President.

June 26.

376   **1799.** "During a severe tempest, resembling in violence the hurricanes of the West Indies, the lightning struck a building directly back of the Court House, then occupied by Isaiah Thomas, in which were stored the types for the 12mo edition of the Bible. The electric fluid, in four distinct veins, pervaded the whole structure, splintering spar and stud, scattering bricks and mortar, and bursting away boards, laths and plastering."—*Lincoln's History*.

June 27.

377   **1862.** Accident at Court Hill.

Three ladies were driving down State street in a chaise, when the horse, taking sudden fright, jumped over the embankment into Main street, landing in a load of shingles which was passing, and breaking its neck. The occupants of the vehicle were buried in the debris, but escaped with slight injuries.

378   **1862.** Causeway through Lake Quinsigamond completed.

Dr. John Green was the first person that passed over. The cost of the causeway, and the improvements in the road leading to it, was $25,997.

June 28.

379   **1818.** Hon. Edward Bangs died, aged 62.

He was born in Harwich, Mass., Sept. 5, 1756. He entered Harvard College in 1773, which he left to participate in the Battle of Lexington. After graduating in 1777, he studied law with Theophilus Parsons, and in 1780, removed to Worcester. During Shays's Rebellion he served under Gen. Lincoln as a volunteer. He was County Attorney for some years; and in 1811, was appointed a Justice of the Court of Common Pleas. He lived on Main street, opposite the Court House.

380   1837.· Brinley (now Grand Army) Hall opened. A concert was given.

This building was erected by George Brinley and Benjamin Butman. The work was done by Mason H. Morse, from plans by Capt. Lewis Bigelow, who also made the plans for Butman Block, south of Elm st.

381   1848. State Convention : Free Soil Party organized.

Hon. Samuel Hoar of Concord was President. An address endorsing the action of Charles Allen and Henry Wilson at the Philadelphia Convention was adopted. Speeches were made by Joshua R. Giddings and Lewis D. Campbell of Ohio; Charles Sumner, Henry Wilson, Charles Francis Adams, and other prominent anti-slavery leaders.

382   1861. Camp Scott, at South Worcester, occupied by the Fifteenth Regiment.

383   1863. [Sunday.] Funeral of Gen. George B. Boomer.

At the Third Baptist Church. The City Government, State Guards and Highland Cadets attended. Gen. Boomer was killed at the Battle of Champion Hill, on May 22d. He was a resident of Missouri; but was brought to Worcester, where his father, the Rev. Job B. Boomer, was then living, for interment. A fine monument marks his resting place in Rural Cemetery.

June 29.

384   1797. "In memory of Capt. John Curtis, who died June 29th 1797 in ye 90 y^r of his age.

"Son of Ephraim Curtis, was born at Sudbury, Sept. 21, 1707. Married Rebekah Waite, probably of Sudbury, by whom he had all his children, viz : John, James, Joseph, Mary, William, Sarah and Tyler. He married for a second wife, Elizabeth Robbins, who was a daughter of Rev. Mr. Prentice of Lancaster. Capt. Curtis for many years kept a public house which was a general rendezvous for all the ministers passing to and fro.

"He held important civil offices, among which were those of Deputy Sheriff and Coroner. He was Captain of a detachment of men from Col. John Chandler, Jr.'s regiment that marched from Worcester on the alarm for the relief of Fort William Henry in 1757. During the revolutionary war, he sympathized with the royal cause, and was a signer of the tory protest of 1774. Also, deemed an internal enemy and disarmed in 1775."—*Inscriptions from the Old Burial Grounds.*

385   **1847.**   President Polk, James Buchanan, Mr. Clifford and Commodore Stewart passed through Worcester on their way to Boston.

The train reached Worcester at 10 A. M.; but owing to some misunderstanding about the time, only a few persons were at the station, some of whom were favored with an introduction.

June 30.

386   **1730.**   "Here lyes interred the Remains of John Young who was born in the Isl of Bert, near Londonderry in the Kingdom of Ireland.   He departed this life June 30th 1730, aged 107."—*Inscriptions from the Old Burial Grounds.*

387   **1841.**   Baptist Church, on Salem street, struck by lightning.

400 school children had gathered with their teachers to arrange for the celebration of the 3d of July; and were dismissed just as the stroke came. About 250 were then inside the building, and nearly all of them were thrown to the floor. 15 or 20 were prostrated in a heap near the door. Two girls had their shoes torn off by the lightning, and one had the bottoms of her feet blistered; but none were seriously injured. No rain was falling at the time.

July 1.

388   **1775.**   Gen. Washington, accompanied by Gen. Charles Lee, passed through Worcester, on his way to Cambridge to take command of the American army.

Washington was also accompanied by his private secretary, Col. Joseph Reed.   At Springfield he was joined by Dr. Church and Hon. Moses Gill, a committee of the Provincial Congress; and the party was escorted from Brookfield by a Worcester company of horsemen, under command of Capt. James Chadwick.   The General and suite were entertained at the Stearns tavern, site of the Lincoln House.

389   **1844.**   Ole Bull's first appearance in Worcester.

At Brinley Hall. He played here for the last time, April 27, 1880. He was born at Bergen in Norway, Feb. 5, 1810; and died there, Aug. 18, 1880.

390 **1855.** Five Cent Savings Bank opened.

391 **1865.** Admiral David G. Farragut arrived in Worcester.
He remained in the city over Sunday.

July 2.

392 **1778.** Execution of William Brooks, James Buchanan,
Ezra Ross and Bathsheba Spooner, for the murder of Joshua
Spooner of Brookfield, husband of the woman.
She was a daughter of Gen. Timothy Ruggles of Hardwick.

393 **1826.** Jeremiah Stiles drowned in Lake Quinsigamond.

He was a man of many and varied talents; a portrait painter of more
than ordinary merit, and a poet of no mean pretensions. His familiarity
with the English classics was wonderful. He painted carriages and
signs for a living.

394 **1836.** American Temperance House, at the corner of
Main and Thomas streets, opened by Eleazar Porter & Co.

This hotel was discontinued after about twenty years, and was then
converted into the present American House Block. Mr. Porter, the
first proprietor, formerly kept the Worcester Temperance House, cor.
Thomas street.

395 **1863.** Rev. Edward A. Walker installed Pastor of the Old
South Church.
He died at Marquette, Mich., April 10, 1866, aged 31.

July 3.

396 **1819.** [Saturday] Republican Celebration of Independence : procession escorted by the Worcester Light Infantry,
Capt. Sewall Hamilton. Oration* by Edward D. Bangs, in
the Old South Church.

397 **1835.** First Passenger Train over the Boston and Worcester Railroad.

The Directors and their friends made the trip from Boston to Worcester and return. On Saturday, the 4th, four trips each way were made,
and more than 1500 passengers carried. For celebration, see July 6.

* Oration printed.

398　1841. [Saturday] Independence celebrated: the Cold Water Army of school children, numbering 1200, with Worcester and other Temperance Societies, held a picnic in the grove back of the hospital.

July 4.

399　1789. Celebrated by a Company of Horse under command of Capt. Denny of Leicester; the Worcester Train of Artillery, Capt. Stanton; and two companies of Militia, Captains How and Heywood; the whole under command of Maj. Phinehas Jones. They paraded the town and were reviewed on the Common. In the evening, the officers and a number of private gentlemen sat down to an elegant entertainment, at which toasts suitable to the occasion were drank.

400　1791. A salute with ringing of bells in the morning. Military parade of company of Artillery, one of horse, and two other companies in complete uniform. An oration* was delivered by Edward Bangs, and an original ode was sung. "After which, the officers and a number of other reputable citizens adjourned to Capt. Heywood's Inn, [site of the Bay State House] where a very handsome but economical entertainment was provided, of which they heartily and sociably partook." —*Spy*. Fireworks in the evening.

401　1792. A salute and ringing of bells. In the forenoon a military parade of the Artillery and two companies of infantry. "A large number of gentlemen met at Heywood's Inn, dined under an arbor built for the purpose, and drank fourteen toasts, with the discharge of fourteen cannon. The day was otherwise spent in social mirth, &c, becoming the occasion."—*Spy*.

402　1793. "In this town a spirit of *manly independence* prevailed. The company of Artillery paraded in the morning; marched up and down the street, exhibiting a very martial and respectable appearance; fired fifteen guns; and were dismissed." A repast was provided at Heywood's tavern, at which toasts were drank.

* Oration printed.

403   1795. Salute and ringing of bells in the morning. A procession formed at Free Masons' Hall and proceeded to the South Meeting House, where "Mr. Joseph Allen, jun. pronounced an oration* fraught with the genuine, manly principles of republican Liberty." The company dined at Masons' Hall.

404   1796. Ringing of bells and display of flags. The company of Artillery, commanded by Capt. Torrey, paraded at 10. At 11, a procession was formed at Mower's tavern, and proceeded to the South Meeting House, where an oration* was delivered by Francis Blake. Dinner at Mower's, with toasts and discharges of cannon.

405   1797. "As Aurora arose smiling she was saluted by 16 discharges from the cannon of the Artillery company. The bells rang and the Flag of the Union was displayed." A procession was formed at Mower's Inn, and proceeded to the South Meeting House, where an oration* was delivered by Doctor Oliver Fiske. A dinner followed. The Worcester Train of Artillery had a supper at Heywood's tavern, and "the anniversary was closed with decent hilarity."

406   1798. Salute and ringing of bells. A procession formed at Masons' Hall and marched to the South Meeting House. The Divine Blessing was invoked by Rev. Joseph Sumner of Shrewsbury; and Rev. Samuel Austin delivered an oration.* "The celebrated song *Adams and Liberty* succeeded the oration, and enlivened the patriotic glow excited by the Day, the Oration, and the particular situation of our Country."— *Spy.*

407   1799. Capt. Healy's Artillery Company escorted the procession to the South Meeting House, where "a select band performed a number of appropriate pieces of Music. . . . . A large assembly of Ladies and Gentlemen were unhappily disappointed of an expected oration. Mr. P[elatiah] Hitchcock, the Orator of the day, on his way from Brookfield to

---

* Orations printed.

K

Worcester, was suddenly seized with a billious colic and was
unable to reach town."

408   **1800.**   Artillery parade.   Oration * by Edward Bangs, in
the North [Dr. Bancroft's] Meeting House.

409   **1801.**   Oration * by Isaac Story of Sterling.

410   **1803.**   Oration * by John William Caldwell, at the South
Meeting House.

411   **1804.**   Oration * by William Charles White of Rutland.

412   **1805.**   Procession escorted by the Artillery Company, Capt.
Slater ; and the Infantry Company, Capt. Flagg.   Oration *
by Daniel Waldo Lincoln.   [Brother of Gov. Levi Lincoln.]

413   **1808.**   "The *Democrats* formed a *great* procession of '*such
as they were,*' and had a very '*magnificent*' oration * delivered
by MAJOR [Estes] HOW, who two years since delivered as
'*magnificent*' a FEDERAL one in Sutton.—Thus we go *up,
up, up !*—and thus we go *down, down, down !* "—SPY.

414   **1810.**   Civic and military celebration.   Oration * by Levi
Heywood.

415   **1811.**   Celebration by young men between 16 and 21.
Oration * by John W. Hubbard, in the South Meeting House.

416   **1812.**   Celebrated by the Washington Benevolent Society
of the County, with a procession escorted by the Light Infantry, Capt. John W. Lincoln.   Oration * by Francis Blake,
in Dr. Bancroft's Meeting House.   Dinner in a building erected for the purpose.

Also celebrated by the Republicans, with a procession escorted by the Artillery.   Oration * by Enoch Lincoln, and an
ode by Edward D. Bangs.   Fireworks in the evening.

417   **1814.**   Celebration by Federal Republicans escorted by
the Light Infantry.   Oration by Edwin A. White, at Dr. Bancroft's Church.

Also a civic procession escorted by the Artillery.   Oration *
by Rejoice Newton, at the Old South Church.

---

* Orations printed.

418   1815. Oration* by Peleg Sprague.

419   1816. Oration* by John Davis, in the Old South Church.

420   1817. Military parade. Oration* by Pliny Merrick, in the Old South Church. An ode composed by Edward D. Bangs was sung by Capt. Sewall Hamilton. A dinner was served in a bower opposite Mr. Hathaway's tavern. Isaiah Thomas presided at the dinner, of which 300 partook.

421   1818. Parade of Worcester Light Infantry. Oration* by Austin Denny, in the Old South Church.

422   1820. Parade of the Light Infantry, Capt. John Coolidge. Oration by Charles H. Warren.

423   1821. Republican celebration, with an address by Henry Rogers, editor of the *National Ægis.*

424   1822. The observance of the anniversary was religious in character. An address was delivered in the Old South Church by Rev. Jonathan Going.

425   1823. Democratic celebration. Oration by Francis B. Stebbins. A dinner, presided over by Otis Corbett, was served in a bower near the hotel of Nathaniel Eaton. The procession was escorted by the Worcester Rifle Corps, Capt. Nathaniel Gates.

426   1825. Celebration by the Light Infantry, with an oration by Richard Hampton Vose, a member of the company.

427   1825. House of Moses Whipple struck by lightning, set on fire, and entirely consumed.

428   1826. First Celebration of Independence under the auspices of the town authorities. The procession, under command of Brig.-Gen. Nathan Heard, comprised the Worcester Rifles, Capt. Thomas Howe ; Worcester Artillery, Capt Elijah Flagg ; and the Light Infantry, Capt. John Whittemore. Oration by Charles Allen. Dinner in the Town Hall, presided over by Isaiah Thomas. Music by the Worcester Harmonic Society, Emory Perry, President.

---

*Orations printed.

429   **1827.** Celebrated by Odd Fellows. Oration in Dr. Bancroft's Church by Thomas Kinnicutt, with a poem by Richard Hampton Vose.

430   **1829.** Military procession of the Providence Light Infantry, Capt. Field ; Leicester Light Infantry, Capt. Joseph D. Sargent ; Worcester Light Infantry, Capt. Charles A. Hamilton ; and Worcester Artillery, Capt. Leonard W. Stowell. Oration in the Old South Church by John Davis, with an ode by Emory Washburn.

431   **1831.** Two processions and celebrations with orations by Edwin Conant and Samuel M. Burnside.

432   **1832.** Two celebrations. The anti-Jackson party listened to an oration by George Folsom, in the Old South Church.

Benjamin F. Thomas delivered an oration in the North Church.

433   **1833.** Celebration under the auspices of the town authorities. A military parade. Oration * by Edward Everett.

Oratorio, directed by Emory Perry, and grand ball at Estabrook's Hotel.

434   **1834.** Whig celebration. Oration by Franklin Dexter, in the Brick Church.

435   **1836.** Whig celebration. Oration by Benjamin F. Thomas.

436   **1837.** Celebrated by the Jackson Democrats.

"In this town the Tories celebrated the success of their efforts in introducing the *Jackson Currency*, and in causing those 'to break' who 'trade on credit.' Their orator was Robert Rantoul, Jr. of Gloucester, Cape Ann, a man of talents worthy of a better cause. . . . . . The dinner was provided at *Brinley Hall*, of which near two hundred and fifty of 'the faithful' partook."—*Spy, July 5.*

437   **1838.** Temperance Festival. Dr. Walter Channing of

* Oration printed.

Boston, Hon. Mr. Hoar of Concord, and Hon. Mr. Lawrence of Belchertown made addresses.

438   1839. Oration at New Worcester by William Lincoln ; Anti-Slavery meeting in Union Church ; and Young Ladies' Picnic at Lincoln Grove.

439   1840. Democratic celebration. Oration by Rev. Orestes A. Brownson.

440   1842. Picnic of the Cold Water Army at Hospital Grove. Temperance Festival of the Washingtonians in the evening. Wendell Phillips made an address at the Town Hall in the morning, and one at Brinley Hall in the afternoon.

441   1843. Picnic of Cold Water Army at Hospital Grove. Washingtonian Festival at Town Hall in the evening.

442   1844. Two celebrations. The Whig "Clay Club" marched to the residence of Ex-Gov. Lincoln, and were presented with a banner by Col. A. H Bullock, in the name of the Whig Ladies of the town. Edwin Conant, president of the Club, replied in an appropriate manner. A public dinner followed, with speeches from Hon. Charles Hudson, Hon. Thomas Kinnicutt and others.

The Democrats celebrated with an oration by George Bancroft in the First Baptist Church, and a dinner at Brinley Hall. Large numbers were present from all parts of the county.

There was also a Temperance celebration.

443   1845. Temperance celebration.

444   1846. Temperance celebration. A display of fireworks in the evening under direction of Dr. Mathew.

445   1847. Fireworks on the Common in the evening, under direction of Dr. Mathew.

446   1850. Parade of the Worcester Light Infantry, Capt. Edward Lamb. The Worcester Guards also paraded. A poem was read at the dinner by Charles Thurber.

447   1851. Free Soil celebration. Oration by John P. Hale.

448   1853. The City Government appropriated $1,500. The military procession of the Jackson Guards, Capt. Driscoll; the Worcester Light Infantry, Capt. Russell; and the Fire Department, was under the command of Chief Marshal Jonathan Day. An oration was delivered by Francis Wayland, in the Old South Church. Dinner in the City Hall.

This was the first public appearance of the Jackson Guards, an Irish company formed the winter before. It was disbanded by Gov. Gardner during the Know Nothing frenzy.

449   1856. The Steam Calliope was played. A floral procession at 8 A. M. was not fully carried out on account of rain. At 10 the mounted Continentals paraded, under command of Charles B. Pratt. At 11 Charles Hersey's "Minute Men" were called by the arrival of the mounted messenger with his cry (feebly given) of *"To arms! War is begun!"* At noon a procession commanded by Gen. George Hobbs, marched through the principal streets to the Common, where dinner was served in a tent. Oration by Homer B. Sprague. At 5 P. M. the Butchers and Provision Dealers paraded in white frocks and caps.

450   1857. Celebrated by two free fights, one at the Providence railroad station, the other in Pine Meadow.

451   1859. Hersey's Minute Men. The messenger was Mr. Lucian Prince, who startled the whole Blackstone valley with his stentorian shout of *"To Arms!"* as he galloped his horse through Main street.

452   1860. Corner Stone of the Free Public Library building laid, with addresses by Mayor Rice and others. A military procession, and a dinner at Mechanics Hall. There was also a balloon ascension.

453   1862. Burlesque parade.

454   1865. Ovation to returned Soldiers. Several arches were erected on Main and other streets. Military parade, which included the veterans, in the forenoon. Trades' procession in the afternoon.

455 **1868.** Studlefunk parade in the morning. Military and civic procession at noon. The Military Division, under command of Col. Robert H. Chamberlain, consisted of six companies of the 10th Regiment, M. V. M.; the State Guards, Lieut.-Col. David M. Woodward; and the Highland Cadets, Capt. L. G. White. The Fire Department, A. B. Lovell, Chief Engineer, formed a part of the procession. There was also a cavalcade, consisting of gentlemen mounted and driving light and fancy teams, and draft horses; in all about 500 horses.

456 **1869.** Corner stone of St. Paul's Church laid.

457 **1870.** Monument to Capt. Peter Slater, one of the Boston Tea Party, dedicated at Hope Cemetery with addresses by Henry Chapin, Isaac Davis, Henry L. Chandler of Lexington, Albert Tolman, Rev. A. P. Marvin and A. B. R. Sprague.

458 **1872.** Studlefunk parade.

459 **1873.** Studlefunk parade.

460 **1876.** Centennial celebration. Studlefunk parade in the early morning. Singing of National Songs by the School children in a large tent on the Common. An extensive military and civic procession in the forenoon, on which occasion the Worcester Continentals made their first public appearance. The Centennial Oration * was delivered in Mechanics Hall by Benjamin F. Thomas; and an Ode written by the Mayor, Clark Jillson, was sung by the pupils of the High school.

461 **1879.** Fatal accident at Lake Quinsigamond. The steamer "Isaac Davis" was boarded by a large and unmanageable crowd, which rushed upon the upper deck, causing the boat to careen over. Five persons lost their lives, and a number were injured.

462 **1883.** Studlefunk procession.

₊ For other Celebrations of Independence, see under dates July 3d, 5th, 6th, 8th and 22d

---

* Oration printed.

July 5.

463   **1790.** [Monday] The anniversary of Independence was celebrated by the Worcester Artillery Company. "At 11 o'clock they paraded before Mr. Mower's tavern, [present location of Clark's block, cor. Mechanic st.] and at 1 o'clock they marched on to the hill by the Court House and fired a national salute ; after which they returned to the place of parade." The officers and several private gentlemen partook of a handsome entertainment, at which toasts were drank. "The company was in complete uniform, and made a very handsome appearance."

464   **1802.** [Monday] Independence celebrated by a parade of the Artillery Company, and an oration * by the Rev. Zephaniah Swift Moore of Leicester.

465   **1805.** Death of William Caldwell, aged 52.
He was Sheriff of the County from 1793 to 1805. His death was caused in part by an attempt at suicide some time before, while suffering under depression of spirits.

466   **1824.** [Monday] Independence celebrated. A procession "numbering 80 in line, including boys," escorted by the Light Infantry, Capt. Artemas Ward.   Oration by William Lincoln.

467   **1830.** [Monday] Independence celebrated. Oration by Peter C. Bacon in Rev. Mr. Abbott's [the Central] Church. At the dinner Isaac Goodwin offered the following toast : "Our venerable townsman, Isaiah Thomas, Esq., *who first promulgated* the Declaration of Independence to the inhabitants of this vicinity from the church and press."

468   **1852.** [Monday] Whig celebration. A large tent was erected on the Common, in which speeches were made by Ex-Gov. Lincoln, Emory Washburn, and Col. Lee of Templeton. The Worcester Light Infantry, Capt. Childs, performed escort duty.

---

* Oration printed.

July 6.

469   1806. . Robbery of the *Ægis* Office.

"In December, 1805, the whole [Ægis] property was attached under a claim growing out of debts of the printer, Samuel Cotting, and the publication suspended. The democratic citizens, roused to exertions, procured new apparatus, which they vested in trustees, and the Ægis again appeared, Feb. 19, 1806, in deplorable dishabille for a time, but soon regained neatness and beauty. A new calamity occurred to interrupt its prosperity. On Sunday, the 6th of July, during the hours of worship, a part of the types were removed, and the sheets, impressed on one side, carried away by Cotting, who, on the next Wednesday, in his individual capacity, sent out the paper in handsome form, while the trustees of the subscription fund were scarcely able to communicate their misfortune. A curious state followed, realizing the confusion of external identity, imagined in the Comedy of Errors. Two papers were published in the same town, on the same day, claiming to be 'the true Ægis.' A contest painful to retrace ensued, disturbing the repose of the village, proceeding almost from words to blows in private discussion, and furnishing subjects for judicial investigation. The good sense of the community, for a time amused by the the bitter feeling of the combatants, and the personal insult degrading pages which should have been devoted to common improvement, at length acted on the source of the commotion, and after a few months of infamous existence, the false print disappeared."—*Lincoln's History*.

470   **1835.** Celebration of the Completion of the Boston and Worcester Railroad.

A procession composed of about 300 citizens of Boston and vicinity, was escorted by citizens of Worcester and the Light Infantry, Capt. Charles H. Geer. A dinner was served in the Town Hall, at which Ex-Gov. Lincoln presided. Speeches were made by the presiding officer; Hon. Nathan Hale, President of the Railroad Company; Hon. Edward Everett and others. During the dinner about 500 ladies were given a ride in the cars to Westborough and return. Hon. Charles Allen was chairman of the committee of arrangements.

471   **1836.** Union Church dedicated.

July 7.

472 **1811.** "In Memory of Capt. William Gates, who died July 7, 1811, Æt. 76.

L

"Capt. William Gates was first sergeant in the company of minute men under the command of Capt. Timothy Bigelow, which marched from Worcester on the alarm at Lexington, April 19, 1775. . Second lieutenant in a company under the command of Capt. Jonas Hubbard, which served three months near Boston the same year. Captain of a company in Col. Jonathan Holman's regiment in the Continental Army. Town Treasurer, 1780-81."—*Inscriptions from the Old Burial Grounds.*

473 **1834.** Foundation of the first Catholic Church in Worcester laid on Temple street.

474 **1869.** Plymouth Church organized.

July 8.

475 **1779.** "Sunday se'night being the anniversary of the Independence of America, the celebration of that day was postponed by the Sons of Freedom, in this Town, until Thursday last. The morning of that day was ushered in by the ringing of bells, the firing of cannon, and a display of the Continental Flag ; at 12 o'clock, thirteen cannon were fired ; in the evening the Court House was illuminated, thirteen rockets were fired, and a display of other fireworks ; greatly to the satisfaction of many respectable and staunch friends to the common cause of our nation, who were assembled at the Court House from this and adjacent towns. Mutual congratulations were given, and a number of toasts suitable to the occasion were drank."—*Spy, July 15.*

476 **1831.** Siamese Twins exhibited in Worcester.

The "Siamese Twins, Chang and Eng were born at Bangesau, on the north-west corner of the Gulf of Siam in 1810. The father was a Chinaman, the mother a Siamo-Chinese woman. They were brought to the United States at the age of 18 by Capt. Abel Coffin, and exhibited throughout this country and Europe ; realized a competence ; married two sisters (mulattoes) in 1842, and settled in Surrey Co., N. C. Each has 9 children. They revisited Europe in 1868-9."—*Drake's Dict. Am. Biog.* The Twins died Jan. 17, 1874.

477 **1856.** Steam Calliope excursion to Fitchburg to attend a Frémont meeting.

The instrument astonished the residents of the County, discoursing music which could be heard for miles as the train moved along. The late

Elijah H. Marshall of Worcester informed the writer that he distinctly heard the music as the train approached Fitchburg, in Lunenburg, where he was visiting, and thought it was a hand-organ close by. The Calliope is an adaptation of the steam whistle to the musical scale, and was invented by J. C. Stoddard of Worcester.

478   1863.   Funeral of Col. George H. Ward.

At the Salem Street Church. The services were conducted by Rev. Mr. Richardson, assisted by Rev. Dr. Hill and Rev. T. E. St. John. The funeral procession included the State Guard, Highland Cadets, City Guard, Members of the Fifteenth Regiment, City Government and ex-Mayors, among whom was the venerable ex-Gov. Lincoln, who marched the whole distance to Rural Cemetery. Morning Star Masonic Lodge also attended.

Col. Ward belonged to the Fifteenth Regiment, and lost a leg at Ball's Bluff. Returning to duty he was placed in command of a brigade, and fell, mortally wounded, in the Battle of Gettysburg.

479   1883.   Death of Hon. John D. Baldwin.

He was born at North Stonington, Conn., in 1810; studied for the ministry and preached for a time, but afterwards adopted journalism as a profession. He was connected with the press at Hartford; was editor of the *Commonwealth* at Boston; and in 1859 purchased the *Spy*. He was a delegate to the Chicago Convention of 1860, and a Member of Congress from 1863 to 1869. Author of two works on archæology, and genealogies of the Baldwin and Denison families.

July 9.

480   1845.   Death of Hon. Daniel Waldo, aged 82.

He was born in Boston, and in 1782, came to Worcester with his father, Daniel Waldo, senior, and engaged in business. Mr. Waldo acquired large wealth, which he liberally dispensed. He built the Central Church and presented it to the society; and also gave the land for Rural Cemetery. In business his habits were exact: he once sent a special messenger to Holden to collect a bill of ten cents. His elegant mansion, occupied by himself and maiden sisters, stood where Mechanics Hall building now is. Mr. Waldo was a member of the famous Hartford Convention.

481   1845.   Rockwell and Stone's Mammoth Circus exhibited on lot at the corner of Main and Chandler streets, present location of Trinity Church.

482 **1871.** French Catholic Church on Park street dedicated. The Society was formed in 1869.

July 10.

483 **1731.** Worcester County erected.

484 **1784.** Rev. Thaddeus Maccarty died. *July, 20*

He was born in Boston in 1721. In his youth he followed a seafaring life, which a delicate constitution induced him to abandon. He graduated at Harvard College in 1739, and three years later was ordained pastor over the church in Kingston, Mass. He was the minister of Worcester from 1747 to his death in 1784.

485 **1784.** House of Bezaleel Stearns, in the Gore between Worcester and Grafton, destroyed by fire.

486 **1856.** Worcester County Frémont Club formed.

487 **1860.** Rosa Bonheur's *Horse Fair* exhibited in Horticultural Hall.

The picture remained here two weeks.

July 11.

488 **1822.** Mutual Fire Society formed.

The Mutual Fire Society had its origin as follows:

"The Hon. Daniel Waldo was a member of the *Fire Club* [i. e. the Worcester Fire Society] formed in 1793, and a by-law of this "Club" provided that no person should become a member of it except by a unanimous ballot. An ecclesiastical fire was, and for years had been, raging in the Old South Church, which set the whole town in a blaze. Mr. Waldo seceded from the Old South Society, and built, at his own expense, a new meeting house, which was completed in 1823, and has been successively called the *Calvinist* Church, the *Central* Church, and often at first, the *Waldo* Church. Gen. Nathan Heard and Hon. John Davis retained their membership in the Old South Church, and were both decided friends of its pastor, Rev. Charles A. Goodrich, a college classmate of Mr. Davis, but the special object of Mr. Waldo's dislike and hostile measures. It so happened, that, without any purpose of involving or affecting ecclesiastical matters, Mr. Heard and Mr. Davis were proposed as members of the old *Fire Club*, and on balloting for their admission, each was *blacked* by the single ballot of Mr. Waldo; and

THE CENTRAL CHURCH.

his exclusion of them from membership led to the formation of the MUTUAL FIRE SOCIETY."—*Manuscript of the Rev. George Allen.*

The original members of this body were Artemas Ward, Austin Denny, Lewis Bigelow, Jonathan Wentworth, Elisha Flagg, Nathan Heard, jun., John Davis, John Coolidge, Stephen Goddard, Joseph Swett, Henry Rogers, Aaron Howe, Sewall Hamilton, Thomas B. Eaton, Simeon Burt, Harmon Chamberlin, Benjamin Howard, Enoch Flagg, Daniel Heywood, William Manning, John F. Clark and John M. Earle.

The following were subsequently admitted: Benjamin Butman, Frederick W. Paine, William D. Wheeler, Gardner A. Paine, William Hovey, Willard Brown, Cyrus Stockwell, Asael Bellows, Francis T. Merrick, Lovell Baker, Luther Burnett, jr., Samuel Harrington, jr., George Day, L. W. Stowell, Zenas Studley, Lewis Lilley, Richard Mills, Albert Brown, Samuel Banister, Alpheus Merrifield. Silas Bailey, James Worthington, Benjamin Porter, William M. Town, William B. Fox, Samuel Congdon and David Wilder.

489   **1840.** First issue of *The North Bend,* a paper published at the office of the *Spy,* in the interest of Harrison for President and John Davis for Governor. It was discontinued after the canvass.

490   **1854.** Worcester County Kansas League formed.

For the encouragement of emigration to Kansas.

491   **1860.** First Public Parade of the Emmet Guards, M. J. McCafferty, Captain.

492   **1863.** Draft in Worcester.

The number drafted in the different wards was as follows. In ward 1, 88; 2, 85; 3, 39; 4, 89; 5, 87; 6, 91; 7, 121; 8, 102.

July 12.

493   **1731.** First Probate Court in Worcester.

494   **1862.** War Meeting in Mechanics Hall.

"The immense losses incurred by our armies on the Peninsula, in the Shenandoah valley, and elsewhere, made it necessary to call for more troops. Accordingly a great meeting was held on the 12th of July, in Mechanics Hall, by request of the Mayor, 'to respond to the call of the Governor, for immediate action in relation to the recruiting of volunteers, to fill up at once the quota of Worcester under said call.' "— *Marvin.* Ex-Gov. Lincoln, Gen. Devens, and Rev. Merrill Richardson spoke.

July 13.

495   1674.   First Indian Deed of Worcester signed.

"A deed of eight miles square, for the consideration of 'twelve pounds lawful money of New England, ... within three months after the date to be paid and satisfied,' was executed, with great formality, . . . by Solomon, alias Woonaskochu, sagamore of Tataesit, and John, alias Hoorrawannonit, sagamore of Packachoag."—*Lincoln's History*. The Indians received, on account, two coats and four yards of trucking cloth.

July 14.

496   1776.   The Declaration of Independence was first read in Worcester.

The messenger bearing the Declaration to Boston was intercepted and a copy obtained, which was read to the people from the porch of the Old South Church by Isaiah Thomas, the patriot printer.

July 15.

497   1835.   Rev. David Peabody installed Pastor of the Central Church.

He was dismissed in 1838, and died while Professor of Rhetoric in Dartmouth College at Hanover, N. H., Oct. 17, 1839, aged 34.

498   1874.   Soldiers' Monument dedicated.

Seven thousand dollars was appropriated by the City Government for the occasion. The procession, under command of Gen. Josiah Pickett, included the City Government and guests, veterans of the war, nearly all the Grand Army posts in the County, with numerous societies and lodges, and the Fire Department. The old State Guard paraded for the last time. At the Monument Hon. Benjamin F. Thomas read an original poem; and addresses were made by ex-Gov. Bullock, Gen. Devens, George Crompton, Esq. and Mayor Edward L. Davis. Vice-President Wilson and Gen. Burnside were present.

The Monument was designed by Randolph Rogers, and cost $50,000.

July 16.

499   1810.   Peter Stowell died, aged 48.

Peter Stowell was a son of Cornelius Stowell who came here soon after the organization of the town, and married a daughter of Palmer Gould-ing, senior. Cornelius Stowell about 1790 took his sons, Peter and Ebenezer, into partnership with him, and began the business of manu-facturing woolen cloths. Jan. 4th, 1793, their shop was burned. In 1804, the sons, Peter and Ebenezer, commenced the weaving of car-pets, plaids, &c., and at one time had six looms of their own invention and construction in operation. They made the first carpets used in the State House at Boston. Peter married Betsey, daughter of Capt. Israel Jenison.

500   **1866.** Reception in Mechanics Hall to James Stephens, the Fenian Head Center.

501   **1870.** Centennial of the *Massachusetts Spy.*

It was observed by a dinner at the Bay State House, followed by re-marks from Hon. J. D. Baldwin, Judge B. F. Thomas, Hon. J. M. Earle, ex-Gov. Bullock, and Messrs. Adin Thayer, C. H. Doe, J. E. Greene, C. H. Woodwell and George Jaques. The next issue of the Spy con-tained fac-similes of the first number published in Boston in 1770, and of the first copy printed in Worcester in 1775.

July 17.

502   **1725.** Indians pursued in Worcester.

See a letter of Benjamin Flagg printed in Lincoln's History.

503   **1776.** The Declaration of Independence first appeared in print in New England, in the *Massachusetts Spy.*

504   **1793.** Death of Hon. Timothy Paine.

He was a son of Hon. Nathaniel Paine of Bristol, R. I., and was born in 1730. Came to Worcester when a child. He was Clerk of the Courts from 1750 to 1774; Register of Probate, 1756 to 1767; Register of Deeds, 1761 to 1775; and a Member of the Executive Council from 1766 to 1773. Appointed one of the Mandamus Councillors in 1774, he was forced to resign by a popular demonstration. He also filled the offices of Selectman, Town Clerk, and Representative. Although of loyal sympathies during the Revolution, he does not appear to have forfeited, in any degree, the esteem of his fellow townsmen.

505   **1854.** First party of emigrants departed for Kansas.

A large number started from Boston, and were joined at Worcester by those belonging in this vicinity.

506   **1860.**   Stephen A. Douglas passed through Worcester.

A large crowd assembled at Washington square, and a salute was fired. Mr Douglas made a brief speech from the platform of the car. He passed through the city again on the 1st of August.

July 18.

507   **1867.**   Death of Hon. Ira M. Barton.

He was born at Oxford, Oct. 25, 1796; graduated at Brown University in 1819; and practised law in Oxford from 1822 to 1834, when he removed to Worcester. He was a Representative, 1830-32, and 1846; State Senator, 1833-4; Elector on the Harrison ticket in 1840; and Judge of Probate, 1836-44. He resided until his death in the Gardner Chandler mansion, opposite the Common.

July 19.

508   **1861.**   Camp Lincoln, at the Agricultural ground, occupied by the 25th Regiment.

509   **1862.**   War Meeting in the City Hall.

Addresses were made by Rev. Mr. Richardson, Major McCafferty and Gen. Devens. A "Committee of Safety" of one hundred was chosen to take in charge the business of recruiting.

July 20.

510   **1818.**   The Elephant *Columbus* was exhibited at Hathaway's Tavern.   Admission 25 cents.

511   **1845.**   Second [Laurel street] Methodist Church formed.

512   **1852.**   Holy Cross College burned.

513   **1854.**   Republican Party organized.

The preliminary organization first attempted in a hall, was adjourned to the Common; Putnam W. Taft was President, and W. H. Harris and Thomas Drew, Secretaries. Permanent organization was effected by the choice of Oliver B. Morris of Springfield as President, with ten Vice-Presidents. Speeches were made by Henry Wilson, Rev. John Pierpont, Theodore Parker and others. Resolutions in stout opposition to the slave power were adopted; and the convention adjourned to meet in September for the purpose of nominating state officers.

THE GARDNER CHANDLER MANSION.

July 21.

514   **1864.** The Fifteenth Regiment arrived home from the war.

It was honored the next day with a grand public reception.

July · 22.

515   **1776.** First Celebration of Independence.

Cannon were fired, bells were rung, bonfires lighted, and the colors of the Colonies displayed. "The Declaration of Independence of the United States was read to a large and respectable body, among whom were the Selectmen and Committee of Correspondence, assembled on the occasion, who testified their approbation by repeated huzzas." A large number repaired to the "King's Arms" tavern, where the obnoxious sign was destroyed, [see ante, No. 26.] and the company partook of a dinner at which toasts were drank.

516   **1802.** "Mrs. Gannet's Exhibition. The Ladies and Gentlemen of Worcester are respectfully informed that Mrs. Gannet, the celebrated American Heroine, who served nearly three years with great reputation in our Revolutionary Army, will, at the request of a number of respectable characters, deliver an Address to the inhabitants of this town, in the Court House, to-morrow, at 5 o'clock, P. M.

"☞ Tickets may be had of I. Thomas, Jun., price 25 cents —children half-price."—*Spy, July 21.*

"Deborah Sampson, who served three years as a soldier in the Revolutionary army, was born in Plympton, Mass., 17 Dec., 1760; died 29 April, 1827. Her poverty and her patriotism led her to enlist in the 4th Mass. Regiment under the name of Robert Shurtleff. She was wounded in a skirmish at Tarrytown; was present at Yorktown; and after the war married Benjamin Gannett, a farmer of Sharon, and received a pension. She published 'Female Review' (12mo, Dedham, 1797), probably written by herself. A new edition, with introduction and notes by Rev. John A. Vinton, was published in 1866."—*Drake's Dict. Am. Biog.*

517   **1847.** Funeral of Capt. George Lincoln, killed in the Battle of Buena Vista, Mexico, February 23, 1847.

The remains arrived from Boston at 11 A. M., under escort of the New England Guards. A procession of military formed on the Common

M

under command of Gen. George Hobbs, and with civic bodies under direction of Col. Isaac Davis, proceeded to the house of ex-Gov. Lincoln, where the remains were received with military honors. The arms of the deceased, with his cap, plume and belt, were placed upon the coffin. His charger, which he rode on the fatal battle field, was led by a corporal of the U. S. Army. The procession moved through Elm, West, Pleasant and Main streets, to the First Unitarian Church, where services were conducted by the Rev. Dr. Hill.

518   1859.   Boiler Explosion at the Wire Works, Grove street.

The large steam boiler, 30 feet long, 4 feet in diameter, and weighing 5 tons, exploded with tremendous force, shattering the engine house of brick, and demolishing walls of buildings adjacent. Several workmen were severely injured. The boiler shot into the air 200 feet and landing in a garden on Lincoln street, 1-4 of a mile distant, rebounded across the street, and entered the earth 4 feet.

July 24.

519   1817.   "New Circus.   Mechanick street, (near the South Meeting House), Worcester.   Mr. West's Stud of performing Horses, for a few nights only.   Boxes, one dollar.   Pit, fifty cents."

520   1845.   First Daily Spy published.

See ante, No. 370.

July 25.

521   1850.   Death of Samuel M. Burnside.

He was born at Northumberland, N. H., in 1783; studied law with Judge Ward of Boston; and commenced practice in Westborough in 1810. He removed to Worcester the same year, where he lived the remainder of his life. His residence for some years was the Jedediah Healy house, between the present American House and Union blocks, on Main street; later, he built the fine residence on Chestnut street, now occupied by his daughters. Mr. Burnside's reputation for learning in his profession was high.

July 26.

522   1809.   First issue of *The Scorpion*.

A virulent political paper, published weekly. Only three numbers were printed.

523 **1826.** Attempt to break the Worcester Bank.

A person representing himself as an agent of the Suffolk Bank of Boston presented bills of the Worcester Bank to the amount of $48,000, and demanded the specie, which was more cash than the bank had in its possession. He was paid in part, and offered a draft for the remainder, which was refused. The next day the property of the bank was attached, but in the meantime provision had been made for the payment of the amount. The action of the Suffolk Bank was in consequence of the refusal of the directors of the Worcester Bank to maintain a deposit with the former for the redemption of its notes. A full account of this affair will be found at page 364 of Hersey's History.

524 **1832.** First Menagerie : Lion, Tiger, etc., exhibited at Central Hotel.

525 **1859.** First Regatta of College crews at Lake Quinsigamond.

Regattas were held here yearly until 1870.

526 **1862.** Great War Meeting on the Common.

The Meeting was called at 11 A. M., and nearly all business was suspended. Addresses were made by Col. Wells of the 34th Regt., Gov. Andrew, John B. Gough and others.

July 28.

527 **1860.** A *Bell and Everett* Flag was displayed at Central Exchange.

July 29.

528 **1861.** Reception of the 13th Regiment.

The Regiment left Boston at 5 P. M., and reached Worcester at 7.15. It was received by four companies from Camp Scott under command of Lt.-Col. Ward; and marched and counter-marched through Main street to the City Hall, where a collation was provided. The Regiment departed at 9.30.

July 30.

529 **1840.** Log Cabin Meeting.

"Gov. Lincoln's speech is spoken of as one of uncommon ability. He fixed the lie on the Palladium man in reference to the charges against himself and Gov. Davis."—*Spy, Aug. 5.*

July 31.

530   1831.   Sunday Evening Concert in the South Meeting House, by the Worcester Harmonic Society, for the benefit of Mr. Emory Perry, the President.   Tickets 25 cents.

531   1873.   Worcester and Shrewsbury Railroad opened.

August 1.

532   1861.   Return of the Worcester Light Infantry from the war.

533   1862.   Great War Meeting in Mechanics Hall under the auspices of the Freedom Club.

August 2.

534   1824.   Corner Stone of Town Hall laid with Masonic ceremonies.

August 3.

535   1775.   "Last Thursday the prisoners who were taken at Light House Island arrived here, under guard, from Head Quarters at Cambridge.   There were twenty-two marines, (including two serjeants and two corporals ; the Lieutenant who commanded the party belonged to the Preston, and was with three others killed on the spot ; seven were wounded), and twelve tory carpenters, (among whom was the infamous Jonathan Hampton of New York), in all thirty-four.   The Saturday following they were according to order, sent from this town to Springfield, where they are to remain for the present."—*Spy, Aug. 9, 1775.*

536   1821.   The West Point Cadets, under command of Major Worth, arrived in town at 6 A. M. on their return from Boston. They encamped on an eminence adjacent to Back (now Summer) st. At 11 A. M. the battalion marched to the hotel of Howe and White. In the evening they were received at the mansion of Hon. Levi Lincoln, and left town at 4 A. M. the next day.

537   **1835.** Visit of the Ancient and Honorable Artillery Company of Boston.

The Company encamped west of the town, and remained three days.

August 4.

538   **1799.** "In Memory of SAMUEL BRIDGE, Deac. of the 2^d Church in *Worcester* In life he exhibited the virtues of the active & useful Citizen, and graces of the pious & cheerful Christian. He was an example of fidelit^y and punctuality. A pattern of decency and order, and A promoter of every plan of public utility· or private benevolence. *Obiit* the 4th of August 1799 *Ætatis* 65.

"Married Mary Goodwin, March 1st, 1757. Lived on the east side of what is now Lincoln street. Was a constable of the town of Worcester. A signer of the royalist protest of 1774. Crier of the Courts from 1779 to 1799."—*Inscriptions from the Old Burial Grounds.*

339   **1864.** National Fast and Great Storm.

340   **1879.** Anthony Chase died, aged 88.

He was born in Paxton, and came to Worcester in 1816. Was in business with his brother-in-law, John Milton Earle, also connected with him in the publication of the *Spy.* He was the first agent of the Blackstone canal; County Treasurer, 1831-65 (succeeded by his son); Secretary Worcester Mutual Fire Insurance Co., 1832-52, and President 1852-79; also connected with other financial institutions. A member of the Society of Friends.

August 5.

541   **1757.** Lord Howe passed through Worcester from Boston ·to New York.

George Augustus, Lord Viscount Howe was the eldest son of the second Lord Howe, born in 1724. He succeeded to the title in 1735. As Colonel of the Royal Americans he was ordered to this country in 1757, and was appointed Brigadier-General in December of that year. He was killed in a skirmish near Ticonderoga, July 6, 1758. Massachusetts erected a monument to his memory in Westminster Abbey.

542   **1851.** Celebration of Emancipation in the West Indies.

Speeches were made by H. I. Bowditch, Parker Pillsbury, William Lloyd Garrison, Wendell Phillips and others.

543   1873. Corner Stone of Piedmont Church laid.

August 6.

544   1803. "Erected To the Memory of LIEU^t BENJ^a STOWELL, who died August 6, 1803. Æ. 73.

"Was lieutenant in Capt. Johnson's company which served under Gen. Amherst in the campaign of 1779. Selectman, 1777."—*Inscriptions from the Old Burial Grounds.*

545   1840. S. G. Goodrich, (Peter Parley), addressed a Harrison meeting.

546   1840. Ladies' meeting in aid of the Bunker Hill Monument building fund.

547   1858. 100 guns were fired and the church bells rung for the success of the Atlantic Cable.

548   1869. Death of Hon. Charles Allen.

He was a son of Hon. Joseph Allen and brother of Rev. George Allen, born in Worcester August 9, 1797. Admitted to the bar in 1818 he practised in New Braintree, but soon returned to Worcester; member of both branches of the Legislature; one of the N. E. Boundary Commissioners in 1842; Judge Court of Common Pleas, 1842-4; Chief Justice of Suffolk Co. Superior Court, 1858-9, and of Mass. Superior Court, 1859-67. In 1848, he dissolved the Whig party at the Philadelphia Convention, by "spurning the bribe" of the vice-presidency offered to Massachusetts; and the ensuing fall was elected to Congress, serving two terms. He was a member of the Peace Convention of 1861.

August 7.

549   1861. A flag was presented to the Fifteenth Regiment by the Ladies of Worcester.

The ceremony took place in the City Hall, and the presentation speech was by the Hon. George F. Hoar, to which Col. Devens made an appropriate response.

August 8.

550   1779. Deacon Chamberlain left the Church on account of innovation in singing.

"Anciently, those who joined in singing the devotional poetry of religious exercises, were dispersed through the congregation. . . . . After the clergyman had read the whole psalm, he repeated the first line, which was sung by those who were able to aid in the pious melody: the eldest deacon then pronounced the next line, which was sung in a similar manner, and the exercises of singing and reading went on alternately. . . . . . By resolution of the town, Aug. 5, 1779, [it was] 'voted, that the mode of singing in the congregation here, be without reading the psalms, line by line, to be sung.'

"The sabbath succeeding, . . . after the hymn had been read by the minister, the aged and venerable Deacon Chamberlain, unwilling to desert the custom of his fathers, rose and read the first line according to his usual practice. The singers, prepared to carry the alteration into effect, proceeded, without pausing at its conclusion : the white-haired officer of the church, with the full power of his voice, read on, until the louder notes of the collected body overpowered the attempt to resist improvement, and the deacon, deeply mortified at the triumph of musical reformation, seized his hat, and retired from the meeting house in tears."—*Lincoln's History.*

551   **1861.**   Departure of the Fifteenth Regiment.

The Regiment participated in the disastrous battle of Ball's Bluff, and also in the battles of Fair Oaks, Antietam, Gettysburg, the Wilderness and others. It arrived home July 21, 1864, with its numbers reduced to 150 men.

August 9.

552 ·   **1856.**   Hon. Henry B. Stanton addressed a Frémont meeting.

August 10.

553   **1731.**   First Inferior Courts in the county.

554   **1808.**   Gen. Moreau passed through Worcester on his way to Ballston springs.

"We have yet to learn what this great General is about in this country; we think the time is not far distant when the mystery will be unravelled. God grant that our fears may prove groundless."—*Spy, Aug. 17.*

Jean Victor Moreau, one of the most eminent generals of France, was born at Morlaix in Brittany, Aug. 11, 1763. Jealous of the ability and power of Napoleon, he was implicated in a conspiracy against him, and in 1804 was exiled to the United States. He lived with his wife at Morrisville, Pa., and at New York until 1813, when he returned to Europe, and co-operated with the allies against France. He was mortally wounded at the battle of Dresden, August 27, 1813.

555   **1835.** Assault on the Rev. Orange Scott. ,

Mr. Scott was delivering an anti-slavery lecture in the Town Hall, when Levi Lincoln, jr., and Patrick Doyle entered and walked directly to the desk. The former seized the lecturer's notes and deliberately tore them in pieces, while Doyle, who was a stout Irishman, laid hold of the lecturer with the intention of dragging him out; several persons interfered and he desisted. The meeting at once dispersed.

August 11.

556   `1805.` [Sunday] Court House struck by lightning.   '

"The lightning touched the front pediment, threw off the shingles, shivered the diamond glass of the large eastern window, shattered the venetian blind, and splintered the style of the door."

August 12.

557   **1812.** Convention of delegates from 41 towns met at Worcester, for the purpose of expressing disapprobation of the war with Great Britain.

August 13.

558   **1846.** Funeral of Bishop Fenwick.

He died in Boston the 10th, and was buried with imposing ceremonies at the College of the Holy Cross, Worcester, on the 13th.

Benedict J. Fenwick was born in Maryland in 1782. Joining the Jesuits, he became President of Georgetown College, and in 1825 was consecrated Roman Catholic Bishop of Boston. He increased the number of churches in his diocese from two to fifty.

August 15.

559   **1862.** Departure of the Thirty-fourth Regiment.

This Regiment was in the battles of New Market, Cedar Creek, Piedmont, Lynchburg, Winchester and others. It was mustered out July 6, 1865.

560   **1875.** [Sunday] Union Railroad Station first occupied.

August 16.

561   **1845.**   Park Street Methodist Church dedicated.

August 17.

562   **1786.**   Johnson Green executed for burglary.

563   **1820.**   Central Church organized.

564   **1861.**   John G. Whittier visited Worcester.

565   **1882.**   Death of Judge Hartley Williams.

He was born at Mercer, Me., and came to Worcester in 1843. He studied law with Hon. F. H. Dewey, and afterwards was his partner for 13 years; was Alderman in 1854; Senator, 1862-3; member of Governor's Council, 1864-5; District Attorney, 1866-8; and Judge of the Municipal and Central District Courts at Worcester from 1868 until his death. He was the first President of the Natives of Maine, and was struck with paralysis while presiding at one of their meetings, March 30, preceding his decease.

August 19.

566   **1839.**   Death of Rev. Aaron Bancroft, D. D.

He was born at Reading, Mass., Nov. 10, 1755; graduated at Harvard College in 1778; and was ordained Pastor of the Second Church in Worcester, Feb. 1, 1786. He married Lucretia, daughter of Hon. John Chandler, the refugee, Oct. 21, 1786. Dr. Bancroft was a Fellow of the American Academy of Arts and Sciences; and was prominently connected with other educational, literary and religious institutions.

567   **1868.**   The Chinese Embassy arrived in Worcester.

Hon. Anson Burlingame, Ambassador; and Chih ta-jen and Sun ta-jen, Associate Ambassadors, and suite, reached here in the afternoon, and remained at the Bay State House over night.

August 20.

568   **1829.**   New Brick Meeting House of the Unitarian Society dedicated.

This building occupied the site of the present edifice on Court Hill. It was destroyed by fire, Aug. 24, 1849.

N

August 21.

569   1735.   Gov. Belcher, accompanied by his Council, passed through Worcester on his way to Albany to hold a conference with the Six Nations.

He was waited on in Worcester by the Justices of the Court of General Sessions, and an address was read by the Hon. John Chandler, to which the Governor replied in a gracious manner.

570   1788.   First issue of the American Herald and Worcester Recorder.

The *Herald* had been published in Boston the seven years preceding, and was continued in Worcester two years and two months. Edward Eveleth Powers, bookseller and printer, was the publisher.

August 22.

571   1774.   Hon. Timothy Paine was forced to resign his office of Mandamus Councilor by a mob of fifteen hundred persons.

He was required to write his resignation, and was then obliged to read it to the people "with his hat off"; after which the crowd withdrew to pay a visit to the Hon. John Murray of Rutland, another Councilor. An interesting account of this affair is printed in Lovell's *Worcester in the War of the Revolution.*

572   1838.   The large Machine Shop of Henry Goulding & Co. on School street, was destroyed by fire.

573   1861.   Ex-President Franklin Pierce in Worcester.

August 23.

574   1824.   Burials on the Common prohibited.

575   1861.   Departure of the Twenty-first Regiment.

This Regiment embarked for North Carolina on the Burnside expedition, and took part in the battles of Roanoke and Newbern. The next spring it was sent to Virginia, and was in the battles of second Bull Run, Chantilly, South Mountain, Antietam, Fredericksburg, the Wilderness and others. It was mustered out Aug. 30, 1864.

576   1877.   Visit of President Hayes.

He was on his return to Washington from the Bennington Centennial, and was accompanied by Mrs. Hayes, Secretary Evarts, Postmaster General Key and Attorney General Devens. The party arrived at 6.50

THE OLD ANTIQUARIAN HALL,

Summer Street.

P. M., and was escorted in procession to the Bay State House. A salute was fired. A reception was held at Senator Hoar's residence and the visitors left the city at 10 P. M.

August 24.

577   1774.   Clark Chandler was forced to obliterate the Tory Protest recorded in the town book.

This protest had been rejected by the Patriots in town meeting, June 20, 1774. (See ante, No. 364.) When the fact that it had been entered upon the records came to light, a storm of indignation was excited, and the town clerk was obliged in open meeting to obliterate the entry with a pen, and was also required to dip his fingers in ink and rub them over the page.

578   1820.   Dedication of Antiquarian Hall, Summer street.

An oration was given by Isaac Goodwin. This building was erected by Isaiah Thomas and presented to 'the society. The main building was 46 feet long and 36 feet wide, with a cupola. Wings were added in 1832, each 28 by 21 feet. This building was, on account of dampness and other considerations, abandoned in 1853, and the collections removed to the new hall on Court Hill.

579   1849.   Unitarian Meeting House burned.

It was erected in 1829 at an expense of $17,000. See ante, No. 568.

580   1872.   Death of George Jaques.

He was born in Brooklyn, Conn., Feb. 18, 1816. After attending Leicester Academy, he entered Brown University and graduated in 1836. For several years he devoted himself to teaching school in Virginia and Massachusetts; later he was engaged in horticultural pursuits and in the care of his estate. He was one of the founders and a prominent member of the Horticultural Society, and compiled the first volume of its transactions. He visited Europe in 1856. In 1871 he presented a lot of about four acres of land to the city as a site for a public hospital; and by his will bequeathed the bulk of his property for the support of that institution. The wishes of the testator were carried out only after much delay and with manifest reluctance by those having the matter in charge.

Many of Mr. Jaques's household effects and family heirlooms were hustled to the auction room and disposed of to a crowd of the curious and vulgar, while his private papers were scattered broadcast. From materials rescued from junk dealers and book-sharks, Mr. Albert A. Lovell compiled and published a memorial volume comprising a sketch of his life and selections from his journals.

August 27.

581   1733.   Millstone Hill granted to the town forever.
See Records of the Proprietors.

582   1781.   "Monday last the Hon John Sullivan Esq., Member of Congress from the State of New-Hampshire passed through this town from Philadelphia.   The celebrated Chevalier John Paul Jones, Capt. in the American Navy, was in company with Gen. Sullivan ; he was also from Philadelphia, bound to the eastward."—*Spy, Aug. 30.*

August 28.

583   1861.   Hon. Joseph Holt, the loyal Kentuckian, passed through Worcester.

August 29.

584   1856.   Lucretia Mott addressed a meeting in Horticultural Hall.

585   1860.   Republican Convention : John A. Andrew first nominated for governor.

586   1868.   Free Public Market opened.
Front street, north side of City Hall.   It was discontinued after a year or two.

August 30.

587   1814.   "*Horrible depravity!*   When the news of the capture of *Washington* reached this town, some of the leading federalists openly expressed their gratification, mingled with a regret that the President was not involved in the destruction of the Capital !"—*National Ægis, Aug. 31.*

588   1854.   First issue of the Worcester Evening Journal.
The Rev. David Higgins was editor until Jan. 1, 1855, when Dexter F. Parker assumed the management of the paper and conducted it in the interest of the "Know Nothing" party.   The last number was dated May 26, 1855.

589　**1862.　Visit of Gen. Corcoran.**

He was given a public reception on the Common at 8 A. M.; a salute was fired and bells were rung. He made a speech to the large crowd assembled, and left for Springfield at 10. "At the depot a large number of ladies availed themselves of the privilege accorded to them by kissing their hero."—*Spy.*

Michael Corcoran was born in Ireland, Sept. 21, 1827, and came to America in 1849. As Colonel of the 69th N. Y. he responded to the call for troops; was taken prisoner at Bull Run, and suffered in rebel prisons for more than a year. After his exchange he returned to duty, and died near Fairfax C. H., Va., Dec. 22, 1863.

August 31.

590　**1863.　Celebration at the opening of the Horse Railroad.**

A salute was fired at New Worcester; addresses were made in Coes's grove by James B. Blake, president of the road; Mayor D. W. Lincoln and others; and an original poem was read by Judge Chapin.

September 1.

591　**1847.　First issue of the Worcester Daily Journal.**

The second number appeared Sept. 15; after that date it was issued daily. It was discontinued in Oct., 1849.

592　**1847.　Henri Herz, composer and first pianist to the King of the French ; and Camillo Sivori, the only pupil of the great Paganini, at Brinley Hall.**

593　**1858.　Illumination and military parade for the success of the Atlantic Cable.**

September 2.

594　**1777.　"On Tuesday arrived here from the northward between four and five hundred prisoners, and yesterday they sat out for Boston, under a strong guard commanded by Lieutenant Colonel Paul Revere."—*Spy, Thursday, Sept. 4, 1777.***

595　**1851.　Powers's "Greek Slave" on exhibition at Flagg Hall.**

596　**1862.　Departure of the Thirty-sixth Regiment.**

This Regiment was in the battles of Fredericksburg, the Wilderness,

Spottsylvania C. H. and others, and performed much hard service and many long marches. It was mustered out June 21, 1865.

September 3.

597 **1823.** First issue of the Massachusetts Yeoman.

This paper was founded by Austin Denny, and was conducted in the interest of the Anti-Masonic party. It was consolidated with the *Ægis* in 1833.

598 **1824.** Lafayette in Worcester.

He arrived at 10 A. M. with a large military escort, and was received by Hon. Levi Lincoln, at his mansion, with an address of welcome, to which he responded. The streets were handsomely decorated with flags and mottoes. After partaking of breakfast and reviewing the troops, Lafayette proceeded on his way at 2 P. M.

599 **1855.** Corner stone of Mechanics Hall laid.

A procession of military and other bodies paraded; Henry S. Washburn delivered an address; and a dinner was served in Agricultural Hall.

600 **1878.** First New England Fair in Worcester.

The Fair was held here annually from 1878 to 1882.

September 4.

601 **1788.** Stone Jail completed.

At what is now Lincoln square. It was judged at the time of its erection to have been "the second stone building of consequence in the Commonwealth; none being thought superior except the Stone Chapel in Boston." It was asserted that it would not need any repairs, excepting the roof, for two or three centuries! It was taken down in 1835.

602 **1850.** Mozart Society formed.

United with the Beethoven Society in Nov. 1866, to form the Worcester Mozart and Beethoven Choral Union, which became, in 1871, the Worcester Choral Union.

603 **1861.** Opening of the Free Public Library Building, Elm street.

604 **1871.** First Passenger Train, Boston, Barre and Gardner Railroad.

September 5.

605   **1786.** Courts prevented from sitting by Shays's insurgents.

606   **1861.** Gen. B. F. Butler spoke on the Common.

He was on his way to Lowell from the seat of war, on a ten days' furlough.

607   **1881.** Death of Samuel F. Haven, LL. D.

He was born in Dedham, Mass., May 28, 1806. Entered Harvard College and completed his course at Amherst. In 1837, he became Librarian to the American Antiquarian Society. He was the author of Historical Address at Dedham, 1836; Archæology of the United States, 1855, published by the Smithsonian Institution; and other works.

September 6.

608   **1774.** The Courts were adjourned by a mob of 6000 men.

They did not resume their functions until after their re-organization in 1776.

609   **1779.** "Monday last the Chevalier de la Luzerne, Minister Plenipotentiary from the Court of France to these States, with his Secretary, attendants, &c., escorted by a party of light dragoons, passed through this town from Boston, on their way to Philadelphia."—*Spy, Thursday, Sept. 9, 1779.*

Anne Cæsar de la Luzerne was born at Paris in 1741. He served in the Seven-Years' War; afterwards was Minister to Bavaria; to the United States from 1779 to 1783; and to London, where he died Sept. 14, 1791. While in this country he conducted himself in a manner that won the affection and esteem of all.

610   **1783.** First issue of the Massachusetts Herald or Worcester Journal.

This was intended as an abridgement of the *Spy*, to be published in quarto form every Saturday. Only four numbers were issued.

611   **1788.** Last Proprietors' Meeting.

612   **1856.** Reception to Hon. Nathaniel P. Banks, Speaker of the U. S. House of Representatives, at the Lincoln House.

613   **1861.** Hon. Horace Maynard, of Tennessee, spoke in the City Hall.

614   **1881.** Yellow Day.

This may be ranked with the celebrated dark day in New England a
century before. Lights were kept burning in the stores, and at times
it was hardly possible to read in the open air. The writer enjoyed the
novelty of eating dinner by lamp-light before an open window at noon-
time. The next day it was found that all the sun flowers had sickened
and died.

September 7.

615   **1864.** Gen. Burnside was serenaded at the Bay State
House, and made a short speech.

616   **1881.** Death of Stephen S. Foster.

Stephen Symonds Foster was born at Canterbury, N. H., Nov. 17, 1809.
Graduated at Dartmouth College in 1838. He became one of the fore-
most anti-slavery agitators of the Garrisonian stripe, and by his methods
brought upon himself much personal abuse and ill treatment. He
married Abby Kelly in 1845. Author of "The Brotherhood of Thieves,
a true picture of the American Clergy."

617   **1881.** Visit of Gen. Sherman.

He arrived at 10 A. M., and was escorted to the N. E. Fair grounds by
military bodies. In the afternoon he visited Grand Army Post 10, and
other institutions. On the morning of the 8th, he visited Shrewsbury
and the tomb of Gen. Artemas Ward.

September 8.

618   **1774.** Convention of Blacksmiths of Worcester County.

Ross Wyman of Shrewsbury was chairman. "They resolved that they
would not, nor either of them, do any work for the *tories*, nor for any
one in their employ, nor for any one who had not signed the non-consumption agreement agreed upon and signed by the Congress at Philadelphia; and requested all denominations of artificers to call meetings
of their craft and adopt like measures,"

619   **1838.** The Rural Cemetery consecrated.

The land was given by Hon. Daniel Waldo. At the consecration, an
address was delivered by Hon. Levi Lincoln, which was printed.

620   **1858.** Great Firemen's Muster.

The Muster lasted three days; 53 companies from other places attended.

September 9.

621   1878.   Death of Gen. Nathan Heard.

He was born in Worcester, March 25, 1790. He succeeded his father as keeper of the Stone Jail at Lincoln square from 1812 to 1822; was afterwards in business with Col. James Estabrook, and with his brother-in-law Geo. M. Rice; also employed at the Custom House in Boston. Representative, 1837-9; Chief Engineer of the Fire Department, 1837-40. He attained the rank of Brigadier-General in the Militia.

September 11.

622   1814.   Worcester Light Infantry and Worcester Artillery marched to Boston to repel British invasion.

They remained in camp at South Boston until Oct. 31, when they returned to Worcester.

623   1874.   State Normal School dedicated.

Addresses were made by Hon. Henry Chapin, Hon. Emory Washburn, Rev. Dr. Miner, Prof. Russell and others.

September 12.

624   1839.   A Negro Boy kidnapped.

Two men named Shearer and Dickinson kidnapped a boy 8 years old, the son of a colored man named John F. Francis. They took the child to Virginia and attempted to sell him, but were arrested and returned to Worcester, tried and sentenced to imprisonment. See ante, No. 45.

625   1843.   Gen. Tom Thumb's first exhibition in Worcester.

He died in 1883.

626   1848.   Abraham Lincoln, of Illinois, addressed a Whig meeting in the City Hall.

September 14.

627   1849.   Young Men's Rhetorical Society organized.

The Society was formed in an upper room of Waldo Block, and was incorporated in 1853.

September 15.

628   1684.   The name *Worcester* was given to the plantation near Quinsigamond Pond.

O

629   **1859.** Benjamin F. Butler nominated for Governor by the Democratic Convention.

September 17.

630   **1674.** John Eliot and Daniel Gookin visited the Indians at Pakachoag.

631   **1757.** Gen. Amherst and his army passed through Worcester.

He was on his way to the westward with an army of 4,500, and was joined at Worcester by a company under Capt. Samuel Clark Paine.

Jeffrey Amherst was born at Kent, England, Jan. 29, 1717, and died Aug. 3, 1797. He was appointed to command the forces in America, and conducted the movements which led to the surrender of all the French possessions in the north. He received many honors, was made a Baron, and became Field-Marshal.

632   **1878.** Mechanics Hall forcibly entered by Butler delegates to the Democratic Convention.

The Democratic State Central Committee having manifested the intention of excluding from the Convention all in favor of the nomination of Gen. Butler, who comprised nine-tenths of the delegates, the Butler men took forcible possession of the hall about 3 A. M., by breaking the lock of a door. The "Silver-Tops" adjourned to Faneuil Hall.

633   **1878.** Dennis Kearney, of California, addressed a crowd at Salem square.

He visited Worcester again, Nov. 4.

September 18.

634   **1857.** Visit and parade of the Woonsocket Guards, and Mechanics Riflemen of Providence.

They were accompanied by Adjutant-General Samuel Cooper of the U. S. army. Gen. Cooper was born in New York in 1796; graduated at West Point; served in Florida and Mexican wars; and was appointed Adj.-Gen. in 1852. He resigned in 1861, and became Adj.-Gen. of the rebel army. He died Dec. 1876.

635   **1872.** Piedmont Church formed.

September 19.

636 **1741.** "Here lies Buried ye Body of William Jenison Esqr. He was born at Watertown April ye 17th 1676, who dec^d Sep^{lm} ye 19th 1741, in ye 66th year of his age.

"He was one of ye Judges for ye Inferiour Court for ye County of Worcester.

"Was Selectman ten years between 1727 and 1741. Representative to the General Court, 1731-2. He gave the land upon which the first Court House was ordered to be built in 1732."—*Inscriptions from the Old Burial Grounds.*

637 **1817.** Long Pond Bridge sunk.

It suddenly gave way and disappeared, leaving but a few shapeless timbers. The bridge was constructed somewhat upon the principle of a wharf, and was intended to form a solid road. It was so far completed that carriages and wagons loaded had passed over it for several days. The disaster was caused by loading it with stones and gravel. Loss, $10,000. The water at this point is 65 feet deep.

638 **1825.** "In memory of JOHN W. HUBBARD, ESQ. *Attorney at Law,* who died Sept. 19, 1825, aged 32 years.

"John W. Hubbard was an adopted son of Rev. Dr. Samuel Austin, . . and nephew of Mrs. Austin. . . . . He was born at Brookfield, Vt.; graduated at Dartmouth College, 1814; and studied law with Gov. Van Ness of Burlington, Vt., and with S. M. Burnside, Esq. of Worcester. . . . . . He delivered the 4th of July oration at Worcester in 1811. . . One of the founders of the Central Church. . . . He owned an estate on Main street, comprising several acres on each side of what is now Austin street."—*Inscriptions from the Old Burial Grounds.*

639 **1838.** Rev. Elam Smalley installed Pastor of the Union Church.

Before his settlement here, Mr. Smalley was nine years associate pastor with Rev. Dr. Emmons at Franklin. Dr. Smalley resigned his charge in Worcester in 1854, and was installed over a church at Troy, N. Y., where he died July 30, 1858. He was author of *The Worcester Pulpit.*

640 **1840.** Worcester County Horticultural Society formed.

September 20.

641 **1753.** "In memory of Jonas Rice Esq, who died Septr 20th 1753, in the 81st year of his age.

"He was the first settler in Worcester, & one of the Judges of the Inferior Court for Worcester."—*Inscriptions from the Old Burial Grounds.*

Jonas Rice came to Worcester from Marlborough in 1713, and for about a year was the only resident of the town. He was the first Schoolmaster (see ante, No. 196.); Selectman and Town Clerk for many years; Judge of the Inferior Court; and Deacon of the Church, 1748 to 1753.

642 **1867.** Death of Calvin Willard, aged 82.

Mr. Willard was Sheriff of the County from 1824 to 1844. He was a native of Harvard.

September 21.

643 **1774.** Convention of Committees of Correspondence of the County.

September 22.

644 **1731.** First Superior Court.

645 **1863.** Celebration of the hundreth anniversary of the erection of the Old South Meeting House.

An introductory address was made by Hon. Ira M. Barton; an historical discourse was delivered by Rev. Leonard Bacon, D. D.; and other interesting exercises followed.

September 23.

646 **1746.** "at a meeting of ye Qualified voters Regulerly assembled on Tuesday Sepr 23 : 1746. . . . .

"This meeting by means of ye Govrners Sending for a Large number of men to oppose ye Suposed french Invasion was Brooke up."—*Early Records.*

647 **1815.** The Great Gale prevailed throughout New England.

648 **1881.** Stephen S. Foster Memorial Meeting.

In Horticultural Hall. Rev. Samuel May presided, and addresses were made by Parker Pillsbury, Lucy Stone, Rev. H. T. Cheever and Wendell Phillips.

September 24.

649 **1745.** "voted that whoever Shall for the future during ye Space of three years . . . . in ye tims of y^e . . Court . . in this Town presume to Run Races on horse back or pace their horses for Tryall in y^e Countrey Road from y^e house of mr. Joshua Eaton to y^e house whear Richard wheelor Lives [the present Main street] Shall forfitt the Sum of Twenty Shillings Lawfull money to y^e use of y^e poare of this Town."—*Early Records.*

650 **1851.** Mademoiselle Teresa Parodi at Brinley Hall.

Tickets $1. She gave another concert in the same hall the 9th of Oct. following; she also appeared in Worcester, Oct. 15, 1856.

September 25.

651 **1727.** "Voted that the Inhabitants of worcester Contribut once a month on y^e Lords Day after Divine Service for the Suport of y^e minister in S^d Town untill a Rate can properly be made according to Contract : Each parson to papre up his 'money & Subscrib his name on ye papre that So accompt may be taken of Each Parsons money and to be Elowed on his Rate when made."—*Early Records.*

652 **1822.** Oratorio by the Handel and Haydn Society of Boston.

In the Old South Church, on the evening of the Cattle Show, and in connection with it.

653 **1868.** Silas and Charles T. James executed for murder.

See ante, No 117.

September 26.

654 **1804.** Worcester District Medical Society organized.

This succeeded the Worcester Co. Society formed in 1794.

655   **1855.**   Baby Show at Flagg Hall.

It continued four days.   Prizes to the amount of $400 were offered, but the managers absconded leaving these and numerous bills unpaid.

656   **1881.**   Funeral Honors to President Garfield.

A meeting was held in Mechanics Hall at noon, and addresses were made by Senator Hoar, ex-Gov. Bullock, Hon. W. W. Rice and others.

September 27.

657   **1803.**   New Court House opened.

658   **1837.**   Gerritt Smith and the Grimke sisters addressed an anti-slavery meeting.

659   **1848.**   First Mechanics' Fair.

In Nashua Hall, present location of the Dean building.   This Fair closed October 3d.   Others were held in 1849, 1851, 1857 and 1866.

660   **1862.**   George Francis Train lectured in Mechanics Hall.

661   **1877.**   Madame Eugenia Pappenheim at the Music Festival.

September 28.

662   **1722.**   First Town Meeting.

September 29.

663   **1790.**   Rev. Samuel Austin installed Pastor of the First Church.

He was born at New Haven, Conn., Nov. 7, 1760.   A graduate of Yale College.   He preached at Fair Haven from 1786 to 1790; at Worcester from 1790 to 1815, when he became President of the University of Vermont, which office he held until 1821; and at Newport, R. I., from 1821 to 1825.   His connection with the church in Worcester was not severed until Dec. 23, 1818.   In 1807, Williams College conferred upon him the degree of D. D.   Dr. Austin was afflicted with melancholia during his last years, and his death, which took place at Glastonbury, Conn., Dec. 4, 1830, resulted from an over-dose of laudanum, administered to afford temporary relief from his sufferings.   His wife was a daughter of Rev. Samuel Hopkins, D. D., of Hadley.

September 30.

664 1796. Rev. Timothy Dwight passed through Worcester.

"Few towns in New England exhibit so uniform an appearance of neatness and taste; or contain so great a proportion of good buildings, and so small a proportion of those which are indifferent, as Worcester."—*Travels, Vol. I., page 366.*

665 1845. New Court House dedicated.

An address was delivered by Chief Justice Shaw. This Court House was built of Quincy granite, and cost about $100,000.

October 1.

666 1801. Corner Stone of the Brick Court House laid by Isaiah Thomas.

667 1839. Western Railroad opened.

First regular train from Worcester to Springfield.

668 1876. Wong Chin Foo lectured in Washburn Hall.

He has since edited *The Chinese-American*, a paper published at New York in the Chinese and English languages.

October 2.

669 1798. Mechanic Street Burial Ground surveyed and laid out.

670 1829. Historical Address delivered before the Worcester County Bar, by Joseph Willard of Lancaster.

671 1852. John W. Lincoln died, aged 64,

He was Selectman, Representative to the General Court, State Senator, and Sheriff of the County seven years from 1844. He presented the Children's Friend Society with the estate at East Worcester, which was for some years the Orphans' Home.

672 1863. Worcester County Musical Society formed.

673 1876. The Ancient and Honorable Artillery Company of Boston celebrated its annual field day in Worcester.

The Company was received and entertained by the Worcester Continentals.

October 3.

674   **1800.   Birth of George Bancroft.**

George Bancroft, distinguished as a historian and politician, was son of Rev. Aaron Bancroft, D. D.   He graduated at Harvard College in 1817, and afterwards studied at German universities.   After his return he was tutor at Harvard, and preceptor of a school at Northampton. About 1835, he entered into politics, allying himself with the Democratic party; wrote many addresses and resolutions, and delivered several orations in its interest; was Collector of Boston, 1838-41; Democratic candidate for Governor, 1844; Secretary of the Navy in Polk's cabinet, 1845; Minister to England, 1846-9; and Minister to Germany. 1867-74.   His History of the United States, begun more than fifty years ago, has just been completed.   The house in which Mr. Bancroft was born is still standing on Salisbury street, near the Highland School, and is now the residence of John B. Pratt.

675   **1859.   Dr. George B. Windship lectured on Physical Culture.**

In Washburn Hall.   Dr. Windship was an enthusiast on the subject of physical training; by practice he was enabled to lift a weight of 2007 pounds.   He died Sept. 12, 1876.

October 4.

676   **1831.   Celebration of the hundredth anniversary of the Incorporation of the County.**

By the Worcester County Historical Society.   A procession marched to the Old South Church, where an address was delivered by Hon. John Davis.   A dinner was served at Estabrook's hotel.

October 5.

677   **1843.   Death of William Lincoln.**

He was born in Worcester, Sept. 26, 1802; graduated at Harvard College, 1822; edited the *Ægis*, and with C. C. Baldwin, published the *Worcester Magazine*.   He was a Representative, 1836-7 and 1841. His History of Worcester was published in 1837.

October 6.

678   **1806.   Thomas Street opened.**

BIRTHPLACE OF GEORGE BANCROFT.

*This street was laid out and given to the town by Isaiah Thomas. The following memorandum was found in one of his almanacs: "1806. Oct. 6. Finished work on the new street. The Selectmen came and surveyed it and laid it out in form. The Light Infantry company, under arms, commanded by Capt. Flagg, marched through it, halted on the bridge, and discharged three vollies. The gentlemen of the street prepared a large tub and two pails full of excellent *punch*, and the Selectmen, at the request of those present, and in conformity to their own proposal, named the street Thomas street. The Infantry company had as much punch as they chose to drink, and all present. Three cheers were given, and the company' marched off."

679   1829.   Harrison Gray Otis and Edward Everett visited the Cattle Show in Worcester.

150 yoke of oxen were driven through Main street. At the dinner speeches were made by the distinguished guests. .

Harrison Gray Otis was a nephew of the revolutionary patriot, James Otis. He was born in Boston, Oct. 8, 1765; graduated at Harvard College in 1783; and by his brilliant talents soon gained a 'high position at the bar; was a Member of Congress, 1797 to 1801; Speaker of the Massachusetts House of Representatives, 1803-5; President of the State Senate, 1805-11; Judge of Court of Common Pleas, 1814-18; United States Senator, 1817-22; and Mayor of Boston, 1829-32. During the troubles with Great Britain, Mr. Otis was a vehement Federalist, and was one of the party of mischievous spirits who were responsible for that egregious political blunder, the Hartford Convention. He died in Boston, Oct. 28, 1848.

680   1857.   Lola Montez lectured in Brinley Hall.   Subject : "Beautiful Women."

Lola Montez, Maria Dolores Porris, Countess of Landsfeld, was born at Limerick, Ireland, about 1820, and died at New York in 1861. At an early age she married Capt. James, and accompanied him to India, but they soon separated. After leading an erratic life in the capitals of Europe, appearing in the streets and theatres as a danseuse and singer, she found her way to Munich, and for some time exerted a powerful influence over King Louis of Bavaria, who made her a countess. She was finally obliged to leave the country. In 1849 she was married to an English gentleman, but his family caused her to be prosecuted for bigamy, as her former husband was living. She came to America in 1851, in the same ship with Kossuth, and appeared in various places in theatres and on the lecture platform.

P

681   1877.   Sale of the old Foster street Depot.

The building was sold by Auctioneer B. W. Abbott, in eight sections as follows: 1, $30; 2, $25; 3, $30; 4, $100; 5, $41; 6, $26; 7, $10; 8, $5.50. Total, $277.50. The frame of the first part of this building was raised May 31, 1835.

October 7.

682   1819.   First Cattle Show in Worcester.

683   1828.   Blackstone Canal opened.

The canal boat *Lady Carrington* arrived from Providence, and was received with firing of cannon and ringing of bells. The last toll on this canal was collected Nov. 9, 1848. A History of the Blackstone Canal, by Israel Plummer, will be found in the first volume of the Collections of The Worcester Society of Antiquity.

684   1835.   Joice Heth, nurse of Gen. George Washington, aged 161 years, was exhibited at Stowell's Railroad House.

Remained here four days; admission 25 cents. This was Barnum's first venture as a showman.

October 8.

685   1818.   "In Memory of Col. BENJAMIN FLAGG who died Oct. 8, 1818, aged 95.

"He commanded a company of minute men which left Worcester, April 19, 1775, on the alarm at Lexington, and attained the rank of Colonel in the Revolutionary Service. Selectman from 1766 to 77 inclusive. An original member of the American Political Society."— *Inscriptions from the Old Burial Grounds.*

Col. Flagg left 4 children, 41 grandchildren and 83 great-grandchildren.

686   1879.   Hon. Zachariah Chandler, of Michigan, spoke at a Republican meeting in the Rink, on Foster street.

He died suddenly at Chicago, Nov. 1, 1879.

October 9.

687   1760.   "We hear from Worcester that on the evening of the 9th inst. the house of Mr. Sheriff Chandler and others of

that town were beautifully illuminated on account of the success of his Majesty's Arms in America."—*Boston News-Letter, Oct. 16, 1760.*

The success referred to was the taking of Montreal by Amherst, Sept. 8, 1760.

688   1816.· Rev. Charles A. Goodrich ordained Pastor of the Old South Church.

He was dismissed Nov. 14, 1820, and afterwards preached at Berlin and Hartford, Conn. He was at one time a member of the Connecticut Senate, and was author of several historical and other books. A brother of Samuel G., widely known as *Peter Parley.* Mr. Goodrich died at Hartford, Jan. 4, 1862, aged 72.

689   1826. President John Quincy Adams visited Worcester.

He remained three days the guest of Gov. Lincoln. The President attended the Cattle Show on the 11th.

690   1867. Gen. Philip H. Sheridan visited Worcester.

He arrived from Boston at 9 A. M., and was received by military bodies and escorted through the principal streets.

October 10.

691   1865. Visit and parade of the Putnam Phalanx of Hartford, Conn.

692   1866. 25th anniversary of the Universalist Church, and installation of Rev. B. F. Bowles.

October 11.

693   1842. First exhibition of the Worcester County Horticultural Society.

At the hall of the Society of Friends, over Joseph Boyden's jewelry store, corner of Walnut street. The exhibition lasted two days.

694   1843. Hon. Richard M. Johnson, of Kentucky, attended the Cattle Show.

Richard M. Johnson was a Representative and Senator from Kentucky for many years, and Vice-President, 1837-41. It has been said that he killed Tecumseh at the battle of the Thames. He died in 1850, aged 69.

October 13.

695   1725. Rev. Isaac Burr ordained.
He was dismissed, March, 1745.

696   1846. John P. Hale spoke in the Town Hall.

697   1878. Death of Hon. Henry Chapin.   ·
He was born in Upton, 1811; graduated at Brown University, 1835; and came to Worcester in 1846. He was Mayor in 1849-50, and Judge of Probate from 1858 until his death.

698   1882. President Arthur and suite passed through Worcester, on their return from the Webster Centennial celebration at Marshfield.

October 14.

699   1740. Visit of Rev. George Whitefield.

700   1867. Parade of the Amoskeag Veterans.

701   1873. Dedication of the Worcester Academy building on Union Hill.

October 15.

702   1823. Dedication of the Central Church and ordination of Rev. L. Ives Hoadly.
Mr. Hoadly was dismissed May 19, 1829. He died at New Haven, March, 1883, aged 92.

October 17.

703   1860. The Prince of Wales and suite passed through Worcester on their way to Boston.
The Prince appeared on the platform of the car, and was greeted with cheers by the large crowd assembled, which he acknowledged by bowing.

704   1865. Death of Dr. John Green.
He was born in Worcester, April 19, 1784; graduated at Brown University, 1804; and practised medicine here more than fifty years. He gave his valuable library to the city, and endowed it.

705　1872.　Remarkable accident on Beacon street.

A horse, attached to a carriage in which was a lady, went over the embankment at the head of Sycamore street, and rolled down 70 feet to the railroad track below. The carriage was broken to pieces, but the woman and horse were not injured.

October 18.

706　1744.　Edward Fitzpatrick executed for murder.

707　1814.　"In Memory of SAMUEL CURTIS Esq. who died Oct. 18, 1814. Æt. 84.

"He was one of the leading Whigs of Worcester during the war of the Revolution. Was one of the committee who reported the constitution and rules of the American Political Society in 1773. In 1776, he was elected magistrate to exercise the powers of Justice of the Peace for the preservation of good order. Was a member of many important revolutionary committees. Selectman, 1766, 75, 90 to 95. Representative to the General Court, 1778 to 1785, 1802, 1804, 1806."—*Inscriptions from the Old Burial Grounds.*

708　1848.　Caleb Cushing spoke at a Democratic meeting in the City Hall, as candidate for Governor.

October 20.

709　1745.　Jeffrey, a Negro, executed for murder.

710　1768.　Arthur, a Negro, executed for rape.

711　1783.　First regular stage from Boston to Worcester.

712　1831.　Daniel Webster and the Everett brothers attended the Cattle Show in Worcester.

713　1849.　Father Mathew, the distinguished Irish temperance agitator, visited Worcester.

He arrived Saturday, 20th; preached at the Catholic church Sunday; and received signatures to the pledge at the City Hall on Monday.

Theobald Mathew was born in Tipperary county, Ireland, in 1790. Educated as a Catholic priest, he performed missionary service at Cork, founded a temperance society, and administered the pledge to 150,000 persons in that place alone. He travelled in the interest of temperance through Ireland, England, and the United States. Queen Victoria bestowed upon him an annuity of £500. He died in 1856.

714 1870. Earthquake Shock.
Buildings were jarred and door bells rung.

October 21.

715 1713. Permanent settlement of Worcester.

716 1742. Jabez Green executed for murder.

October 22.

717 1783. First stage from Hartford to Boston passed through Worcester.

October 23.

718 1789. President Washington passed through Worcester.
He arrived early in the morning, and was received with salutes of cannon by the Worcester Artillery. The President took breakfast at the "United States Arms," [now Exchange Hotel], and then proceeded on his way to Boston.

719 1850. Woman's Rights Convention.

October 24.

720 1732. "In answer to ye Petition of ye Revd mr. Isaac Burr, Voted that ye Sum of Twenty Pounds be assessed according to Law on the Inhabitants and Estates of ye Town of worcester to be payd to mr. Burr, which Sum the town Cherfully grant and earnestly Desire that he Lay ye Same out in purchising an addition to his Library."—*Early Records.*

721 1812. The American Antiquarian Society incorporated.
"The persons named in the act were gentlemen eminent for their learning and ability, who stood high in the confidence of the public, viz: Isaiah Thomas, Levi Lincoln, Harrison G. Otis, Timothy Bigelow, Nathaniel Paine, Edward Bangs, John T. Kirkland, Aaron Bancroft, Jonathan H. Lyman, Elijah H. Mills, Elisha Hammond, Timothy Williams, William D. Peck, John Lowell, Edmund Dwight, Eleazer James, Josiah Quincy, William S. Shaw, Francis Blake, Levi Lincoln, Jr., Samuel M. Burnside, Benjamin Russell, Thaddeus M. Harris, Redford

Webster, Thomas Wallcutt, Ebenezer T. Andrews, Isaiah Thomas, Jr., William Wells." Of these, Isaiah Thomas was the master-spirit, and on its incorporation, he presented the Society with his private library; and in 1820, erected a building for its reception. The Society removed to its present quarters in 1853. The library now comprises over 70,000 volumes; the aggregate of the several permanent funds is about $80,000. The interior of the library is arranged with fine effect; and the cordial welcome extended, and absense of red tape, make it a pleasant resort for the student or antiquary.

722 **1864.** Dale Hospital occupied.

This building, now the Worcester Academy, was erected for a medical college, and afterwards used for a female seminary. It was occupied by the Government, during the latter part of the Rebellion, as a hospital for disabled soldiers. It was formally inaugurated, Feb. 22, 1865.

October 25.

723 **1770.** William Lindsay executed for burglary.

724 **1847.** Providence and Worcester railroad opened.

725 **1871.** City Hospital opened.

In the Abijah Bigelow house, corner of Front and Church streets.

October 26.

726 **1864.** Trial and presentation of the organ in Mechanics Hall.

October 27.

727 **1868.** Gen. O. O. Howard lectured in Mechanics Hall.

October 28.

728 **1859.** Benjamin F. Butler spoke in the City Hall as Democratic candidate for Governor.

He was elected 23 years later.

October 29.

729 **1868.** David R. Locke, otherwise *Petroleum V. Nasby*, lectured in Mechanics Hall. Subject : "Cussed be Canaan."

October 30.

730   **1852.** Charles Francis Adams spoke at a grand rally of
the Free Democracy.

731   **1854.** Butman Riot.

Asa O. Butman, Deputy United States Marshal, came to Worcester for
the purpose of seizing an escaped slave named William H. Jankins.
The friends of the slave gathered in large numbers, and in the attempt
to get Butman out of the city by a few who interposed between him
and the mob, he wellnigh became a victim of its fury. A graphic account of this affair, by Rev. Albert Tyler, will be found in the first volume of the Collections of The Worcester Society of Antiquity.

October 31.

732   **1722.** Rev. Andrew Gardner dismissed.

He was the first Minister of Worcester, settled in 1719. Afterwards
preached in Lunenburg, and died in New Hampshire, at an advanced
age, in 1793. He was noted for his eccentricities.

733   **1793.** Samuel Frost executed for murder.

734   **1805.** Nathaniel Mower's hat shop burned.

735   **1842.** John B. Gough signed the pledge.

He was reclaimed by Joel D. Stratton, Sunday evening, Oct. 30, 1842;
and the next evening took the pledge, at a temperance meeting in the
Town Hall. Stratton was at that time employed by Thomas Tucker,
who kept the American Temperance House. He died Nov. 4, 1860.
A sketch of his life, by Rev. Horace James, was published.

736   **1844.** Swiss Bell Ringers at Brinley Hall.

737   **1861.** Departure of the Twenty-fifth Regiment.

This Regiment embarked with the Burnside expedition; took part in
the battles of Roanoke Island and Newbern; and performed service in
North Carolina until the fall of 1863. The next spring and summer
the Regiment saw hard service, passed through Drewry's Bluff, Cold
Harbor and other battles, and spent the hot months before Peters-
burg. It arrived home, (excepting a portion that re-enlisted the winter before), October 13, 1864.

November 1.

738 1851. Joshua R. Giddings addressed a Free Soil meetin;
in the Foster street Depot.

He spoke in the City Hall in the forenoon. It was charged that the
Whigs engaged the hall for the evening to keep the Free Soil men
out, and the use of the depot was tendered. Over 3000 were present.

739 1851. Hon. George S. Hillard addressed the Whigs at
the City Hall.

740 1859. Dr. J. G. Holland lectured on "Art and Life," in
Mechanics Hall.

741 1875. Dr. Hans Guido Von Bülow at Mechanics Hall.

One of the most eminent pianists of the present time. He was born
at Dresden, Jan. 8, 1830. Was assisted by Liszt and Wagner, and
made his first appearance as a pianist in 1852. His compositions are
numerous and of a high order. He is now an inmate of an insane
asylum. He married a daughter of Liszt from whom he was divorced;
she then became the wife of Wagner.

November 2.

742 1865. Edwin Forrest at the Theatre.

He appeared the evenings of the 2d and 3d, in Richelieu and Lear.

November 3.

743 1856. Dr. Charles Robinson, the Free Soil Governor of
Kansas, addressed a meeting at the City Hall.

744 1859. Henry D. Thoreau lectured on John Brown, at
Washburn Hall.

November 4.

745 1777. Gen. Burgoyne and Hessian prisoners captured at
Saratoga passed through Worcester.

746 1829. Worcester Lyceum formed.

747 1833. Henry Clay visited Worcester.

Q

He was the guest of Gov. Lincoln. On the 5th, he was welcomed at the Town Hall by Hon. John Davis, and made a speech. In the afternoon he visited Millbury. On the 6th he departed for Hartford.

748   **1848.   Charles Sumner spoke at a Van Buren meeting.**

Sumner, at this time, was disfavored by the so-called *respectable* element of the state, on account of his association with the Abolitionists. After Mr. Sumner had been elected Senator, the following editorial appeared in the Boston Daily Advertiser of April 25, 1851.

"It is unnecessary for us to add anything to what we have already said of the disgraceful character of the coalition by which this object has been accomplished. It is the grossest outrage upon the feelings of the majority of the people of the state, by a combination of two minorities, which we have known to be perpetrated in any of the states of the Union. We regard this event as a most unfortunate one for the reputation of the state, and one which must paralyze its influence in the councils of the Union."

The above remains one of many evidences of the political wisdom and foresight of the Old Whig Party of Massachusetts.

" O Time ! whose verdicts mock our own,
The only righteous Judge art thou ! "

749   **1849.   Father Mathew's Mutual Benevolent Total Abstinence Society formed.**

November 5.

750   **1788.   Two Camels, late from Arabia, arrived in town with their keeper.**

November 6.

751   **1848.   Daniel Webster spoke three hours at the City Hall for Taylor and Fillmore.**

Just before the meeting, a Free Soil procession paraded the streets with torches, and Webster noticed the large number it comprised. Gov. Lincoln remarked that they were mostly boys. "But these boys will soon be men," replied the great statesman. Webster was brought here at this time to denounce Charles Allen, (then running for Congress on the Free Soil ticket), but he made no allusion to him. The next day, Judge Allen was triumphantly elected over the Whig incumbent, Hon. Charles Hudson.

November 7.

752   1714. Birth of the first male child in Worcester : Adonijah, son of Jonas Rice.

753   1781. Celebration of the surrender of Cornwallis, news of which was received the evening before.

November 8.

754   1861. First appearance in Worcester of Brignoli.

Signor Pasqualino Brignoli, long a favorite tenor with the American public, was born at Milan in 1832.

755   1882. Christine Nilsson at Mechanics Hall.

Tickets, $1., $2. and $3. A small audience attended.

November 9.

756   1871. Samuel L. Clemens, otherwise *Mark Twain*, lectured in Mechanics Hall on "Artemas Ward."

November 10.

757   1778. Wedding of Hannah, daughter of Sheriff Gardner Chandler, and John Williams of Boston.

Hepsy Hemmingway said she well recollected the marriage, "for Burgoyne's Band came down from Rutland, and played before the house of Sheriff Chandler all that evening."

758   1858. Frederick Warren shot.

Mr. Warren was City Marshal. He received a fatal wound by the accidental discharge of a revolver in the hands of Henry W. Hendricks, a deputy sheriff of Charleston, S. C., and died on the 13th. A public funeral was held on the 15th.

November 11.

759   1779. Robert Young executed for rape.

He was one of the Convention troops.

760   1868. Worcester Free Institute of Industrial Science dedicated.

November 12.

761   **1861.** Funeral of Lieut. John William Grout.

He was a member of the 15th Regiment, and was killed in the battle of Ball's Bluff, Oct. 21, 1861.

762   **1866.** Clara Barton lectured on "Work and Incidents of Army Life."

763   **1866.** Maggie Mitchell in *Fanchon*, at the Theatre.

764   **1883.** Heavy Gale : car with nine passengers blown from the track of the Worcester and Shrewsbury railroad. No one was injured,

November 13.

765   **1849.** Peace Celebration : reception to Elihu Burritt on his return from Europe.

November 14.

766   **1864.** Lynde Brook water let on.

November 15.

767   **1865.** Blind Tom at Mechanics Hall.

He was born a slave in 1838. He possessed little intelligence, but could perform the most difficult pieces of music on the piano after once hearing them.

768   **1871.** Batchelder's painting of the *Battle of Gettysburg* exhibited at Horticultural Hall.

November 16.

769   **1775.** Post Office established in Worcester.

Isaiah Thomas was appointed Postmaster, and held the office until 1801. His successors have been : James Wilson, 1801 to 1833; Jubal Harrington, 1833 to 1839; Maturin L. Fisher, 1839 to 1849; Edward W. Lincoln, 1849 to 1854; Emory Banister, 1854 to 1861; John Milton Earle, 1861 to 1867; and Josiah Pickett, the present incumbent, appointed in 1867.

770   1795. Worcester Association of Mutual Aid in Detecting Thieves formed.

November 17.

771   1777. "On Monday last arrived here, and on Tuesday proceeded on their way to Boston, under an escort of light dragoons, his Excellency the President of the Continental Congress [John Hancock] and his lady."—*Spy*, *Nov. 21.*

772   1883. Corner Stone of the first Swedish Methodist Church in New England laid at Quinsigamond.

November 18.

773   1776. "Last Monday passed through this town under guard, about 120 tories brought from Phillips Manor and places adjacent ; 30 of whom were enlisted under the infamous Major Rogers and taken in a late skirmish."—*Spy*, *Nov. 20.*

November 19.

774   1857. Park Benjamin read a poem entitled *Hard Times.*

775   1869. Edwin Booth in *Hamlet.* at the Theatre.

November 21.

776   1786. Court closed by Shays's insurgents.

777   1837. John Bell of Tennessee, William J. Graves of Kentucky, and Gov. Edward Everett, addressed a meeting in the Unitarian Church, and were given a supper at the Worcester House.

John Bell was born near Nashville, Tenn., in 1797, and died there in 1869. He was a Member of Congress, 1827-41 (Speaker one term); Secretary of War, 1841; Senator, 1847-58; and Union candidate for President, with Edward Everett as Vice-President, in 1860. William J. Graves is chiefly noted for having killed Jonathan Cilley in a duel, in 1838. He was a Member of Congress from Kentucky, 1835-41; and died in 1848, aged 43· Edward Everett, eminent as an orator, scholar, and politician, was born at Dorchester, Mass., Oct. 11, 1794. He was educated at Harvard and German universities, and became pastor of the Brattle Street Unitarian Church in Boston. Finding politics more congenial to his talents than preaching, he entered Congress in 1825, and served ten years; was Governor, 1835-40; Minister to England, 1841-5; President of Harvard University, 1846-9; Secretary of State, 1852-3; and Senator, 1853-4. He died Jan. 15, 1865.

778 · 1877. Railroad tracks removed from the Common.

November 22.

779   1864.   Celebration of the completion of the Water Works.

The dam at Leicester was inspected; a meeting was held in Mechanics Hall, with addresses by Mayor D. W. Lincoln and others; and the Fire Department, City Officials, etc., headed by the Cornet Band, proceeded to the corner of Main and Myrtle streets, where the new works were tested in the presence of a large assembly.

November 24.

780   1737.   Hugh Henderson, alias John Hamilton, executed for burglary.

The first execution in this county.

781   1836.   Rev. Jonathan E. Woodbridge installed first Pastor of the Union Church.

782   1870.   Olive Logan lectured in Mechanics Hall.

783   1871.   Peace Meeting to celebrate the Washington Treaty.

In Mechanics Hall. Addresses were made by Mayor Edward Earle, Hon. P. Emory Aldrich, Rev. J. B. Miles, Hon. Amasa Walker and Elihu Burritt.

November 25.

784   1761.   "In memory of Deacon Nathaniel Moore, who died Nov'' 25 : A. D. 1761 Aetat 84 years.

"Came from Sudbury. Was the third settler of the town of Worcester, arriving here in 1715 or 1716. He was Deacon of the First Church from its foundation, and remained in that office until his death. Was Selectman of the town for eleven years between 1722 and 1740. Town Treasurer, 1725 and 1731. He married Grace Rice, sister of Jonas Rice, the first permanent settler. She died in 1768, aged 94 years."— *Inscriptions from the Old Burial Grounds.*

785   1862.   Departure of the Fifty-first Regiment.

This Regiment enlisted for nine months, and spent most of its time of service in North Carolina.   It arrived home July 21, 1863.

November 27.

786   1843.   The Town was authorized to purchase Bladder Pond for a water supply.

787   1868.   Gen. Kilpatrick lectured in Mechanics Hall on "Sherman's Grand March to the Sea."

Judson Kilpatrick was born in New Jersey in 1836, and graduated at West Point in 1861.   He was an efficient cavalry officer in the Rebellion, and attained the rank of Major General.   In 1865 he was appointed Minister to Chili, and died there Dec. 6, 1881.

788   1883.   Matthew Arnold, the English philosopher and critic, lectured on "Literature and Science" at Horticultural Hall.

Admission $1.   About 300 attended.

"Mr. Matthew Arnold after his recent visit here being asked by a Boston friend how he liked Worcester, said he did not enjoy himself very much; that, having no invitations, he thought he would try an American inn, and found one named the "Bay Horse," where, as they only had noon dinners, he could get nothing to eat but cold oysters.   Our hostelry, famed in political and other annals, would scarcely be recognized by its best friends under the very English name of the "Bay Horse."—*Spy, Jan. 11, 1884.*

November 28.

789   1873.   Rev. Newman Hall, of London, lectured in Mechanics Hall.

He preached at the Union Church on the afternoon of Saturday, Nov. 29th.

790   1875.   Remains of Vice-President Wilson arrived in Worcester.

Henry Wilson died at Washington, Nov. 22, 1875.   His remains arrived here Sunday morning at 4.50, and remained until 8.30.   At 7, the City Guards escorted the City Government and distinguished citizens to the Union Station.   The remains were placed in the vestibule and viewed by a large number.

791   1883.   Serious accident on the Boston. Barre and Gardner railroad, near North Worcester.

A car on the afternoon inward bound train left the track and rolled down an embankment. A large number were injured; two fatally.

November 29.

792 **1856.** New England Non-Resistance Convention.

W. L. Garrison, S. S. Foster, Rev. Adin Ballou and others spoke.

793 **1859.** Alvan Allen killed on the railroad.

He was run over between Front and Mechanic streets, near the Foster street station. Mr. Allen came from Sturbridge in 1835, and was mail agent between Worcester and Hartford until the opening of the Western railroad. Afterwards in the grocery business and a dealer in pianos. He was a member of the Common Council; City Marshal, 1853; and Auditor in 1858.

November 30.

794 **1850.** George Thompson, the celebrated English Abolitionist, visited Worcester.

His presence in Boston in 1835 was the cause of the Garrison riot. Mr. Thompson was again in Worcester during the Rebellion.

December 1.

795 **1856.** Worcester School of Design and Academy of Fine Arts established.

Located on the upper floor of Clark's block, corner of Mechanic and Main streets. The school was maintained about five years.

796 **1862.** Rev. William R. Huntington ordained Rector of All Saints Church.[1]

[1] He resigned Dec. 1, 1883, to become Rector of Grace Church, New York City.

December 2.

797 **1675.** "This day all the houses in Quonsukamuck were burnt by the Indians."—*Increase Mather*.

The buildings had been deserted by the inhabitants, through fear of Indian attack, some time before.

798   **1801.**   First issue of the National Ægis.

This paper was founded to sustain the principles of Thomas Jefferson against the misrepresentation and abuse of the Federalists of Massachusetts. It was published until 1833, when it was merged with the *Yeoman.* It was edited successively by Francis Blake, Edward Bangs, Levi Lincoln, Samuel Brazer, William Charles White, Enoch Lincoln, Edward D. Bangs, Pliny Merrick, William Lincoln, Christopher C. Baldwin and William N. Green. The paper was re-established in 1838, and in 1857 was merged with the *Transcript,* which was succeeded by the present *Gazette.*

799   **1879.**   Death of Rev. William M. Parry.

He was a native of Nottingham, England, and came to this country in 1872, and was acting Pastor of the Old South Church for about two years. He possessed genius, learning and ability, but was erratic and eccentric. He organized the Tabernacle Church in 1874. In his will he made special request that his friends and the newspapers would make no mention of his decease or of anything concerning him, which was disregarded.

December 3.

800   **1881.**   New City (or Jaques) Hospital opened.

December 4.

801   **1862.**   A deserter was shot on the Common.

A company of about 100 deserters from Fort Independence passed through Worcester in the steamboat train in the evening. Two or more jumped from the train, and one, named Michael Farrel, aged 22, was fired at by the guard and shot through the body. He died on the 6th.

802   **1873.**   Fall of a building on Main street.

The north wall of the unfinished building opposite the Old South Church, belonging to Gross and Strauss, fell about 5 A. M., in consequence of the freezing of the mortar. The low wooden building adjoining, occupied as a music store, was entirely demolished.

803   **1873.**   Edward Jenkins lectured in Mechanics Hall on "The England of to-day."

He is the author of "Jinx's Baby."

R

December 5.

804   1837. Convention of Ministers of Worcester County called
to express sentiments against slavery.

This was brought about principally by the efforts of Rev. George Allen,
and clergymen of various denominations to the number of about eighty
attended. A "Declaration" offered by Mr. Allen was considered too
radical, and the Convention adjourned to meet the 16th of the following January, when a manifesto (substantially Mr. Allen's) was put
forth which had great influence in shaping public sentiment on the
slavery question.

805   1873. Bret Harte lectured on "The Argonauts of '49."

December 6.

806   1786. Arrival of Daniel Shays.

The leader of the insurgents arrived from Rutland with 350 men which
with those already here, increased his force to nearly 1000. The Court
House had been seized by the rebels on the 3d, and they remained in
possession of the town about a week.

807   1817. "Col. Ebenezer Lovel Died Dec. 6, 1817, aged 88
years.

"An officer in the Revolutionary war. Was ensign in the company of
Capt. Benjamin Flagg, which left Worcester on the alarm at Lexington
in 1775. Was one of the 'Committee of Inspection' chosen in 1774 to
examine from time to time the merchants and traders of the town, and
see that no imported goods were offered for sale in violation of the
'solemn league and covenant.' Selectman, 1778, 79, 84. Representative to the General Court, 1777. One of the original members of the
American Political Society."—*Inscriptions from the Old Burial Grounds.*

808   1875. Prof. Richard A. Proctor, the English astronomer,
lectured in Plymouth Chapel on "Other Worlds and other
Suns than ours."

He subsequently lectured several times in Worcester.

809   1882. Transit of Venus.

It was observed in Worcester at the High School, State Normal School,
Free Institute and Worcester Academy. At the High School, Principal Roe obligingly gratified a large number of persons with a view of
the phenomenon, which will not occur again until the year 2005.

[Street.] (left side)   **[West.]** (right side)

- No 13 Tyrus Rice
- No 12 Josⁿ Whitney
- No 11 Nathˡˡ Moore
- No 10 Nathan Perry
- No 9 Joseph Clark Jun.
- No 6 James Nichols
- No 7 John Chandler assignee of Asa Flagg
- No John Mahan
- No 5 John Chandler Esq
- No 14 Daniel Ward
- No 15 Josiah Harrington
- No 16 Francis Harrington
- No 17 Jacob Hemingway
- No 47 Jonathan Stone
- No 46 Gershom Comfort Rice
- No 45 James Putnam Esq
- No 44 Thos Shearpe
- No 43 John Boyden
- No 42 Daniel Boyden
- No 41 Samuel Curtis
- No 40 David Bancroft
- No 39 John Chaddick
- No 38 Thomas Rice
- No 37 Thomas Parker
- No 36 John Mower
- No 35 Asa Moore
- No 34 Ebenezer Lovell
- No 4 Thomas Wheeler
- No 3 James Brown
- No 2 Gardiner Chandler
- No 1 Nathanael Adams
- No 18 John Chandler Esq
- No 19 David & Abel Heywood
- No 20 Elisha & Robert Smith Barber
- No 50 Daniel Towne Pew
- No 49 James McDaniel
- No 51 John Curtis
- No 52 Josiah Brewer Esq
- No 53 Luke Brown
- No 21 Robert Barber
- No 22 Jacob Chamberlin
- No 23 Elisha Smith Jr
- No 24 Isaac Gleeson
- No 25 Samuel Miller
- No 57 James Goodwin
- No 56 Matthew Gray
- No 55 Benjˡ Flagg
- No 54 William McFarland
- No 61 Robert Gray Jun.
- No 60 Jonᵃ & David Dike
- No 59 Joseph Blair
- No 58 Isaac Moore
- No 33 Timothy Paige Esq
- No 32 John Chandler Esq
- No 31 Samuel Mower
- No 30 Jacob Holmes
- No 29 Israel Jennison
- No 28 Samˡ Hunt assignee of Thomas Cowdin
- No 27 Ezekiel Flow
- No 26 Josiah Pearce

[15 feet]

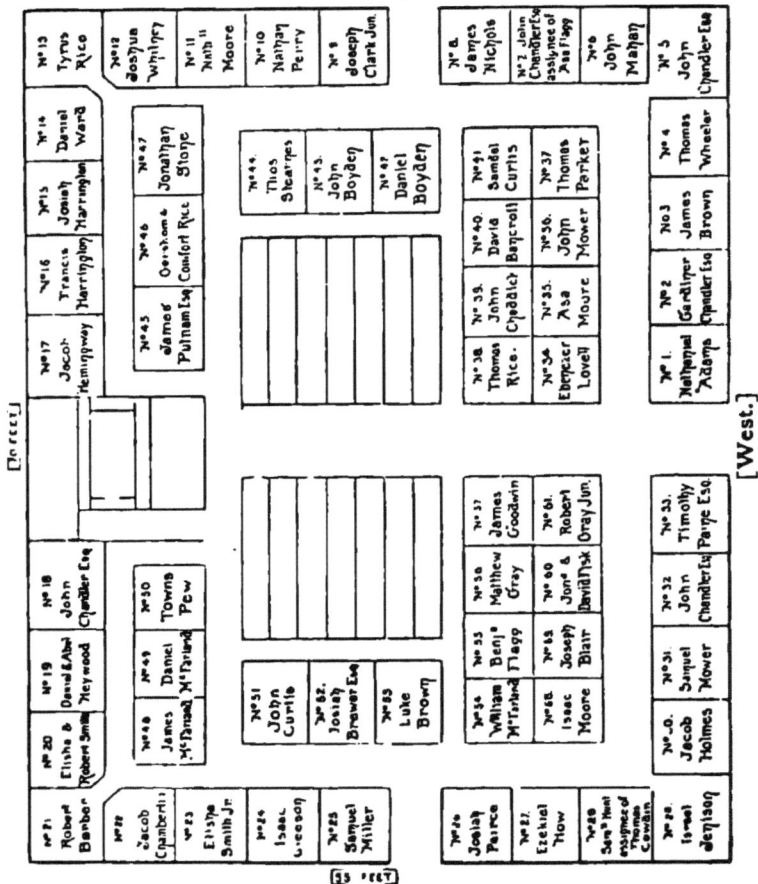

PLAN OF THE MEETING HOUSE, 1764.

December 7.

810   **1825.**   Horace Carter executed for rape.

811   **1869.**   Death of Dr. Benjamin F. Heywood.

He was a son of Hon. Benjamin Heywood of Worcester, born April 24, 1792. He graduated at Dartmouth College in 1812; took the degree of M. D., 1813; and practised here many years.

December 8.

812   **1763.**   The Old South Meeting House first used for religious purposes.

813   **1829.**   Anti-Masonic Convention at the Court House.

814   **1872.**   Free Public Library opened Sunday.

"And God said, Let there be light."

December 9.

815   **1812.**   First Baptist Church formed.

816   **1819.**   "In Memory of Mr. DANIEL BAIRD who died Dec. 9, 1819, aged 77.

"Married Jane Smith, January 8th, 1768, and kept the Baird Tavern. "He was sergeant in Capt. Benjamin Flagg's company that marched from Worcester on the alarm at Lexington, April 19, 1775. Sergeant in Col. Crafts' regiment of artillery, 1776. Private in Capt. David Chadwick's company that marched to Hadley on the alarm at Bennington, Aug. 28, 1777.

"Mr. Baird held the office of Selectman for five years commencing with 1785, and was a member of the American Political Society."— *Inscriptions from the Old Burial Grounds.*

Mr. Baird was concerned in Shays's Rebellion, and was confined in Boston Gaol, March 5, 1787.

817   **1819.**   Worcester County Anti-Slavery Convention.

At the Court House. It was called to take action to prevent the further introduction of slavery into new states.

December 10.

818   **1775.**   "On Sunday last the lady of his Excellency General

Washington, and the lady of General Gates, with their attendants, passed through this town on their way to Cambridge." —*Spy*.

819   1851. ·Jenny Lind, assisted by Otto Goldschmidt, Signor Belletti and Mr. Joseph Burke, gave a concert at the City Hall.

> Tickets $2., $3. and $4. Every seat was taken. A large number gathered about the building to catch such notes as might escape through the walls. This was her farewell concert in Massachusetts.
>
> "Jenny never sang better, or gave better satisfaction."—*Spy*.
>
> She occupied rooms at the Worcester House.

820   1856. B. L. Batchelder of Sutton drew a barrel of beans on a hand-sled from Sutton to Worcester, in fulfillment of an election wager with T. W. Short of Worcester.

> The bet was made on the result of the presidential contest : Buchanan vs. Fremont. Mr. Batchelder, wearing snow-shoes, left Sutton at 10 A. M., and arrived at the lower end of Green street at 3.30, where he was awaited by a large concourse. A procession was formed, headed by a band of music, and proceeded through Main street to the Bay State House, Mr. Short riding in a barouche. Here the beans were delivered to Mr. Short, Mr. Z. K. Pangborn making the presentation speech, to which Mr. Calvin E. Pratt responded, speaking from the top of an omnibus. An immense crowd blocked the street. A bean supper was served to a large company.

December 11.

821   1823. David Brown, a Cherokee, delivered an address in the Old South Church, in aid of a mission to establish schools among the Cherokees of the Arkansas.

822   1873. Thomas Nast lectured on ·"Caricature."

December 12.

823   1848. Salem Street Church dedicated.

824   1855. William M. Thackeray lectured in the City Hall.

825   1874. Death of Alexander H. Wilder.

He was born in Lancaster, and came to Worcester in 1823 as a clerk in the Registry of Deeds, and succeeded Artemas Ward as Register in 1846, retaining the office until his death.

December 13.

826   1835.   First Episcopal Service in Worcester.

827   1866.   John G. Saxe read a poem entitled "Love," at Mechanics Hall.

December 15.

828   1717.   First recorded death in Worcester : Rachel Killough, daughter of John and Jean Killough.

829   1861.   Hon. Daniel S. Dickinson of New York lectured in Mechanics Hall on "The Union, its perils and hopes."

December 16.

830   1870.   Gas Explosion resulting in the death of Mayor James B. Blake.

Mayor Blake was Superintendent of the Gas Works, and going in the evening with the foreman, who carried a lighted lantern, to inspect some repairs in the purifying room, a severe explosion ensued in consequence of the escape of gas from an open stopcock. The building was demolished and the Mayor and his attendant severely burned and bruised. Mr. Blake died about 36 hours after the accident. A public funeral was held in Mechanics Hall on Thursday, Dec. 22.

December 18.

831   1848.   Worcester and Nashua Railroad opened.

December 19.

832   1768.   "Here lies Buried ye Body of Gershom Rice, who died Dec^m ye 19th A. D. 1768, in ye 102^d year of his age.

"Gershom Rice was son of Thomas, who was the third son of the emigrant, Edmund Rice, who came from England and settled in Sudbury in 1639, and afterwards removed to Marlboro', where he died May 3,

1663. Gershom Rice was the second settler of Worcester, coming here in 1715. Selectman, 1724, 27, 31, 33, 36, 46. Town Treasurer, 1736. It was at his house that religious services were first held in the town."
—*Inscriptions from the Old Burial Grounds.*

833   **1838.** Rev. Seth Sweetser installed Pastor of the Central Church.

December 20.

834   **1810.** "ERECTED In memory of EPHRAIM MOWER Esq. who departed this life Dec. 20, 1810, Æt. 62.

"Married Thankful Hersey of Leicester, and kept the hotel which stood near the corner of Main and Mechanic streets, on the site now occupied by Clark's block. Was one of the original founders of the Second Parish Church in Worcester, organized in 1785, and at the first meeting of the members of the parish called for the election of officers in 1789, Mr. Mower was chosen collector. Selectman from 1790 to 1810 inclusive. Representative to the General Court from 1806 to 1810, and Crier of the Courts from 1800 to 1807."—*Inscriptions from the Old Burial Grounds.*

December 21.

835   **1882.** First issue of the New England Home Journal.

December 22.

836   **1825.** Edmund Kean, the celebrated English tragedian, remained in Worcester over night.

He passed through Worcester on the 20th, and attempted to play in Boston on the evening of the 21st, but was prevented by riotous demonstrations. He left Boston and arrived in this town, well armed, on the night of the 22d, and departed for New York the next morning.

Edmund Kean, one of the greatest lights of the English stage, was born in London in 1787, and achieved his greatest triumphs at the Drury Lane theatre. His principal characters were Othello, Shylock, Richard III., and Sir Giles Overreach. He visited this country twice. Dissolute habits hastened his death, which occurred May 15, 1833.

837   **1858.** Rev. Rush R. Shippen installed Pastor of the Church of the Unity.

December 23.

838   **1859.**   Free Public Library established by ordinance.

839   **1873.**   First exercise of the Veto Power by the Mayor.
Mayor Jillson vetoed an order authorizing the laying out of a street (the Boulevard) over Elm Park.

December 24.

840   **1824.**   "Hancock Arms" or Butman tavern burned.

841   **1839.**   George Combe, the eminent Scotch Phrenologist, lectured in Worcester.

842   **1868.**   Paul B. Du Chaillu lectured on African Travels.

December 26.

843   **1865.**   Hon. Schuyler Colfax gave a lecture descriptive of his tour across the Continent.

December 27.

844   **1773.**   American Political Society formed.

845   **1859.** A Steam Fire Engine was exhibited on the Common.

December 28.

846   **1841.**   Second Baptist Church organized

December 30.

847   **1868.**   Death of Ichabod Washburn.
He was born in Kingston, Aug. 11, 1798; came to Worcester about 1820 and engaged in the manufacture of lead pipe and wire; and in 1834 established a wire factory on Grove street—the foundation of the present extensive works of the Washburn and Moen Company.

848   **1871.**   New High School Building dedicated.

849   **1881.**   Eulogy on President Garfield by Hon. George F. Hoar.

December 31.

850   **1875.**   Illumination in honor of the Centennial Year.

GENERAL INDEX.

GENERAL INDEX.

The figures refer to the Paragraphs.

☞ Many titles which properly have *Worcester* or *Worcester County* prefixed to them, as Worcester Light Infantry, Worcester Palladium, Worcester County Horticultural Society, etc., are indexed' as Light Infantry,

www.ingramcontent.com/pod-product-compliance
Lightning Source LLC
Chambersburg PA
CBHW030849270326
41928CB00008B/1292